It's *Your* Time

To Mike and Lynn

Have a wonder-filled future - I know you will!

It's *Your* Time

Information To Get You Ready For a Great Retirement

Second Edition
Revised and Updated

Donna McCaw

Toronto
www.bpsbooks.com

First published in 2011 by
BPS Books
Toronto and New York
www.bpsbooks.com
A division of Bastian Publishing Services Ltd.

Second edition published by BPS Books, January 2017

ISBN 978-1-77236-039-4

Cataloguing-in-Publication Data available from Library and Archives Canada.

Cover: Gnibel
Typesetting: Daniel Crack, Kinetics Design, kdbooks.ca

Printed by Lightning Source, Tennessee. Lightning Source paper, as used in this book, does not come from endangered old-growth forests or forests of exceptional conservation value. It is acid free, lignin free, and meets all ANSI standards for archival-quality paper. The print-on-demand process used to produce this book protects the environment by printing only the number of copies that are purchased.

To my parents, Floyd and Audrey McCaw,
who encouraged me to get an education and a career.

To my son, Arthur, my nephews, Scott and Harrison,
and my nieces, Shauna and Jenna,
who have great adventures ahead of them.

And to my readers, for taking the time
to prepare for retirement.

Contents

Introduction: Looking Forward to Retirement 1

Section One: **Getting Started**

Retirement: True or False? 5

The Process of Retiring 7

Pre-retirement 7

Celebration 8

Honeymoon 8

Reorientation 8

The New Normal 9

Slow-Go 9

No-Go 9

Boomers Hit Retirement 10

The New Retirement 12

Retirement Snapshot 12

Reasons for Retirement 13

What Planning for Retirement Involves 13

Put Your Team Together 14

Retirement: The Final Frontier 14

Retirement Plans and Expectations 16

Timing 16

Finances 16

Health 16

Leisure Time 16
Relationships 17
Research 17
Anticipating Problems 17
Your Retirement Planner 18
Balancing Your Wheel of Life 19
Threat or Opportunity? 19
The Role of the Job 20
Employers and Retirement Planning 21
Mourning the Loss of Your Career 22
Look Before You Leap 23
Who's in Charge? 24
To Retire or Not to Retire 25
Phased Retirement 26
Retirement Shock 26
Getting Started Checklist 28

Section Two: **Finances**

Financial Tips and Facts 31
Financial Planning 31
Getting Prepared 33
Using Retirement Calculators 33
Timing Is Everything 34
Canada Pension Plan Revisited 34
Inflation Bites! 35
Get Your Financial Picture in Focus 35
Ownership of Assets 36

Your Net Worth 37
Your Income and Expense Statement 38
So How Much Do I Need, Anyway? 39
Sources of Income 40
Financial Considerations 41
Longevity Risk 41
Lifestyle 42
Fate and Other Factors 42
Financial Shifts at Retirement 43
Now What? 43
Income Realities 44
What You Need to Know 45
Figure Out Your Future Income 46
Pension Envy 47
Cushioning Surprises 47
Options and Ideas 48
Delayed Retirement 48
The Age of Aging 49
Protect Your Estate 50
Where Is Your Information? 51
Climb Out of the Debt Hole 52
Wham Bam Money Scams 52
Top Ten Scams 53
Financial Abuse of Seniors 54
Living Out of Country 54
Your Home 55
Aging in Place by Renovation and Design 56
Snowbirding 57

Financial and Legal Ducks in a Row 58
Getting Advice 58
What About Insurance? 59
A Word to Women on Retirement and Finances 61
Guerrilla Frugality 64
Retiring from the Farm 65
Philanthropy and Legacy 66
Financial Checklist 68

Section Three: **Health and Wellness**

Health Tips and Facts 73
Health Is the Wild Card 74
Healthy Aging 76
Health Downsides of Retirement 77
For Better Health, Find Your People 77
Top Health Issues Affecting Women 78
Cardiovascular Disease 79
Breast and Lung Cancer 79
Type 2 Diabetes 79
Musculoskeletal Diseases 80
Mental Health 80
Menopause 81
Suggestions for Boosting Metabolism 81
The "P" Word 82
Women and Long-term Health 82
Top Health Issues Affecting Men 82
Cancer 82

Heart Disease and Stroke 83
Type 2 Diabetes 83
Suicide 84
Erectile Dysfunction 85
Take Care 85
The Aging Process 86
Carpe Diem! 88
Risk Factors and Health 89
Countering Health Risk Factors 89
Two "S" Words ... Sex and Seniors 90
The Scourge of Dementia 91
Recognizing Dementia 92
Exercise the Gray Matter 93
Work It Out 94
Food for Thought 94
Caregivers 95
Financial Considerations for Health Care 96
Health-care Checklist 98

Section Four: **Lifestyle**

Six R's of Retirement 101
Time to Be Inspired 102
Recreation/Leisure Tips and Facts 103
Demographics 105
The First Two Years 105
The Power of a Positive Attitude 107
Passive vs. Active Leisure 108

Your Legacy . . . 109
Creative Retirement Ideas . . . 110
Dreams Do Come True . . . 111
Making Dreams Real . . . 112
Volunteering . . . 113
The Art of Finding Your Volunteer Group . . . 113
Questions About Volunteering . . . 114
A Word to Men on Retirement . . . 115
Lifestyle Checklist . . . 117

Section Five: **Relationships**

Relationship Tips and Facts . . . 121
Yikes, There's a Spouse in the House! . . . 121
The Importance of Staying in Touch . . . 124
Gray Divorce . . . 125
Heads Up . . . 126
A Word to Widows and Widowers . . . 127
On Your Own . . . 128
Relationship Checklist . . . 130

Section Six: **Transitions**

Tansitionability Tips and Facts . . . 133
Lost in Transition . . . 133
Identity Crisis . . . 134
Secrets of the Successfully Retired. . . . 136
Walking the Talk . . . 137
How to Manage the First Year . . . 138

Attitude Is Everything 139
It's Not Just Betty White 141
Advice from Those Who've Gone Before 142
Regrets – I've Had a Few 142
Your "I'm Retired Now" Introduction 143
Retirement – Putting It All Together 144
Have a Dream 145
Transitions Checklist 146

Section Seven: **Resources**

Online Resources 149
Books for Further Research 151
Films to Inspire Thinking About Aging and Retirement 152

Acknowledgements 155
About the Author 157

Introduction

Looking Forward to Retirement

The earlier you imagine and begin to plan your retirement, the easier your transition to retirement will be.

Your plan may lead you to various endeavours, like pursuing educational enrichment, getting involved at the civic or community level, volunteering abroad, starting a business, or hiking through natural wonders.

When you own your decisions, you are the architect of your life. Think back to the crossroads times in your life – those important transitional moments – and recall the options you sorted through. Retirement presents a whole new set and experience of options to consider and choose. It is yet another transition in your life, and one that requires active management.

This book is designed to give you a heads-up on the main issues and decisions you need to consider and act on as you prepare for *your* retirement. As you read on, explore options from a broad, anything-is-possible perspective. As in planning a canoe trip, over-prepare and then go with the flow. Follow your bliss.

It's Your Time guides you through the most important components of retirement planning, with sections on Getting Started, Finances, Health and Wellness, Lifestyle, Relationships, Transitions, and Resources. The information throughout the book encourages you to approach retirement with knowledge, imagination, and confidence to make creative, rational, and informed decisions.

Retirement is a gift of modern times: a gift of time and freedom you can maximize and thoroughly enjoy. It is a process – a transition that is really a series of transitions unique to each person. Indeed, planning a creative and realistic retirement while you are still employed will help you develop a positive vision of your future. This book will help you plan the retirement that's right for you.

It is a mistake to regard age as a downhill grade toward dissolution. The reverse is true. As one gets older, one climbs with surprising strides.

~George Sand

Section One

Getting Started

RETIREMENT: TRUE OR FALSE?

1. Early retirement can be detrimental to health, triggering serious illness, or even death. T / F
2. Researchers have found that a spiritual practice of some sort is one way to ensure better health in later life. T / F
3. The majority of Baby Boomers say they plan to work full or part time after retiring. T / F
4. Working women whose partners make no effort to coerce them into retirement are at least four times happier in retirement than those who feel coerced. T / F
5. Married men view their retirement as an opportunity to get to know their wife better. T / F
6. Canadian public health workers report increased drug use and sexual activity in the 65-plus population resulting in side effects like sexually transmitted infections (STIs). T / F
7. We continue to grow brain cells and interconnectivity in the brain in later life. T / F
8. Being in the sandwich generation can put you in a big squeeze. T / F
9. Retirement triggers a change in life interests, activities, and values. T / F
10. Those who think the most about retirement are the most pessimistic about it. T / F

For the answers, see next page.

ANSWERS to Retirement Questions

1. **True**
   Involuntary retirement is especially dangerous to physical and mental health, but inactivity and depression can also be problematic to retirees.
2. **True**
   Social connections and a faith practice have positive effects on health, including the positive outlook and sense of belonging that may come as a result.
3. **True**
   These may be bridge jobs or businesses that supplement income and maintain social connections, sense of purpose, and mental stimulation.
4. **True**
   The decision to retire is individual as well as relational.
5. **False**
   Sorry!
6. **True**
   Be careful of drug dependency and little blue pills, and use protection.
7. **True**
   Keep on learning and growing!
8. **True**
   Children are dependent longer and parents are living longer.
9. **False**
   We stay who we are. Priorities may change, but there is continuity in interests, activities, and values.
10. **False**
    The better prepared you are, the better choices you make.

THE PROCESS OF RETIRING

Many Boomers are uncomfortable with the word "retirement." They associate it with "put out to pasture" or "over the hill" or "now I have to admit that I am aging." Some experience real retirement anxiety prior to this major life transition.

Be assured, retirement today is not what it used to be. Many keep working in some capacity, start a business, or try a whole new way of living. It is an opportunity to reinvent and redefine both lifestyle and identity. Both passion and purpose need to be a part of this new stage. The Boomer generation is blessed to have the opportunity for a very rewarding retirement.

PRE-RETIREMENT

The anticipation can be pleasant or anxiety inducing depending on that attitude to retirement. Some are enthusiastic and dive into dreaming, planning, imagining, and looking forward to the freedom from work. Others avoid the topic altogether. Some are in complete denial. Both avoidance and denial can leave such people in a state of near paralysis. No decisions. No planning. No idea of timing, assets, or resources, or clues about what to do with all that extra time.

This is the time to play with options, dream big, and communicate with friends and family about ideas for the future. Do some research and experimentation. Examine options. Build a team of trusted advisors. Get financial ducks in a row. Try out new interests, hobbies, and courses, and set some priorities. Make some new friends outside work. Be prepared for the ending of this career, and look for the beginning of the next stage of life.

Be aware that many do not control the timing of their retirement, because of a health issue or a pink slip, buy out, or "ease out." Even though mandatory retirement is no longer in place, terminations do happen regularly. A 2014 study by Sun Life found that 69 per cent of Canadians did not stop working on the date that they had planned. Some of those would have chosen to continue working while others got an unpleasant surprise. That is why you need a Plan A and a Plan B.

Almost 20 per cent of Canadians say that they will never retire. Some of them are correct, but most are not. Another 60 per cent say they have not saved enough to retire. You have choices to make so that you do not find yourself ill and out of a job with little in the way of assets and savings.

Check with CRA (Canada Revenue Agency) for tax benefits and credits.

Find out about your retirement income like the Old Age Security payment and your Canada Pension Plan by contacting Service Canada to find out your timing and options. Check with your employer if you do have a pension. If it is a defined benefit, figure out how much it will be, whether it is joint and last survivor or single life, and when it will start. If it is a defined contribution, figure how best to convert it to an RRSP, RRIF, or annuity.

CELEBRATION

Have one! Do not just slip out the back, or leave on Friday and not show up on Monday. People want to say goodbye. This is the time for handshakes, thank-you cards and speeches, farewells, memories shared, a thoughtful gift, perhaps, and a retrospective of your career that can be public or private. The option is available to have some input with your employer, the social committee, or family about that celebration. Design your last message to and memory of your place of work unless you hate it so much you just want out.

Take some time to plan or design a more personal or private celebration with a few friends, family, with a special party, trip, or dinner. Mark this transition how you choose to, but, by all means, do mark it. Just like a graduation, a wedding, a baby shower, this transition is a major life shift. You want to feel and experience that change has happened. It is a rite of passage that deserves recognition for the profound transition that it is.

HONEYMOON

This part of the process can last a few weeks, months, or even a couple of years. This is the euphoric experience of the freedom to do what you want and when you want to do it. The bag of rocks is off your back, and time expands. The world is popping with possibilities. Retirement plans reach fruition by taking a special trip, relocating, renovating, or relaxing. Now you set your schedule and routines and can throw out the alarm clocks! Each day is a treasure to be opened and explored. All those preretirement daydreams can now come true.

REORIENTATION

Now that the honeymoon is over and every day is no longer a holiday, it is time to head into a new life as the old one fades. As one fellow phrased it, "There was a time I realized I had gone from a legend to nobody pretty fast. I had nothing to talk about with my old buddies from work. They were not really interested in what I was up to now." This may sound familiar as life at work moves on without you.

For some, real life crashes on the rocks of the daily grind. Now what? Feelings of restlessness, disappointment, and confusion can signal the beginning of the reorientation time. Something seems to be missing or out of kilter, or maybe the reality of reinventing a whole new life is intimidating. Some marital strain may rock the boat as all that togetherness is just a bit too much. Many may be seeking more mental stimulation or looking for a new project or challenge.

This is where self-awareness and self-assessment come to the fore. Keep it simple by getting to the basics like who, what, when, where, and why. Who are the people to spend time with, doing what, how often, in what place, and why? Think about personality, experience, skill sets, and interests. Figure out what creates happiness, excitement, and engagement. Go on a quest to get needs met. Figure out how to structure time and find a sense of purpose. This can be daunting; a counsellor or a coach may be the person to help you with navigating the process to find that new focus.

THE NEW NORMAL

Retirement is a series of transitions, experiments, and adjustments. At this point, the retiree could have new social networks, a newly negotiated relationship with family, a routine in place, and a predictability that is comfortable and secure.

Time to design the new life, find new social circles, and reinvent a new identity to a degree. Keep an eye on moods and happiness levels and adjust as needed. This is part of active retirement sometimes referred to as the go-go stage. Enjoy it while you can.

SLOW-GO

At some point, the travel bug may not bite so much. Aches and pains or a health issue may mean a slow-down. There may be caretaking of another family member, a health issue, or concerns about finances. The routines and schedules may be more ingrained. As one of my favourite authors put it, "I had no idea at this stage of my life that most of my time would be taken up with maintenance. I am just trying to hang on to what I've got like my body, home, and money."

NO-GO

By this stage, a medical condition or two or more could mean time is spent at home or in a home. Maybe you need support or care. The world may have shrunk considerably to a room or two.

Each stage of the process requires some preparation from finances to self-awareness.

Preparation can head off confusion, alienation, relationship problems, depression, and needless unhappiness.

BOOMERS HIT RETIREMENT

- Canadian Boomers were born from the late 1940s to the early 60s, went to work starting in the mid to late 60s to the 80s, and started reaching 65 in 2012. About a thousand Canadians a day turn 65
- They are working longer for the income and to address concerns about the effects of a 20-35 year retirement like medical expenses
- Boomers in Canada make up about one-third of the population
- They value independence, hard work, education, adventure, and resilience
- They are concerned about health issues, jobs, stress levels, finances, and relationships
- Financial priorities include paying down debt including credit cards and mortgages
- They control over half the wealth in the country and will inherit even more
- Only about one-third have a retirement plan and only half of those feel ready to retire
- Half intend to work in some form after they retire to make extra money, keep busy and engaged, or service debt. Many want more flexibility in their employment with options for time off, work sharing, longer holidays, or a move to a less stressful position
- About 10 per cent say they will never retire, and another 10 per cent have started or plan to start a business
- Many are concerned about a "purpose gap," searching for a sense of meaning to their lives in retirement
- Many are tech savvy and innovative. They resent the retirement word and passive image of retirement. They will take the seniors discount – but call them one at your peril!
- Many are squarely in the sandwich generation between adult children who may need their help and increasingly frail parents who need care
- Concerns about the silver tsunami include the effect on the health-care system

with cancer, heart issues, arthritis, dementia, and all the ills an aging generation can present. That demand has started and will likely continue until the mid-2030s. Other concerns are about housing and services, pensions, pharmacare, and the falling ratio of taxpayer to dependents

- Advertisers are targeting this generation of Zoomers, as labelled by Moses Znaimer and the CARP organization
- Politicians also cannot ignore a large generation in which 70 per cent actually vote
- The sex, drug, and rock-and-roll generation is using Viagra, has the fastest-growing divorce rate, is getting STIs at an alarming rate, is taking on average five prescription pills a day, is seeing the legalization of marijuana, and is listening to Neil Young, Leonard Cohen, and the Rolling Stones, as well as Arcade Fire and The Sheepdogs
- Common money drains are educating and supporting adult children, servicing mortgage and other debt, and lifestyle costs
- Many plan to renovate to age in place or move with aging in place in mind
- Canada ranks fifth behind Sweden, Norway, Germany, and the Netherlands as having the oldest average age population. By 2030, the world's population is projected to be 16 per cent over age 60
- About 250,000 Canadians retire each year; Statistics Canada projects that to climb to 400,000 retirees per year
- Of those retired, 56 per cent have no debt, 79 per cent own their home, 52 per cent say their standard of living is about the same, and 24 per cent say it is down somewhat
- 61 per cent of 50-plus retirees have RRSPs, 56 per cent have mutual funds, and 47 per cent have TFSAs
- The most common debt is a line of credit
- Retirement is set to change when this generation redesigns, redefines, expands, and experiments with what is possible at this stage of life

THE NEW RETIREMENT

- A mix of education, work, leisure, fitness, lifestyle experiments and changes, travel, and volunteering
- It is not a cookie-cutter experience. Everyone is different in their approach to and experience of retirement
- Baby Boomers represent 30 per cent of the Canadian population, making retirees a large segment of the voting population
- Average life expectancy has increased to 83 for women and 78 for men, while many people are retiring sooner, making the retirement period longer than in any other period in history. These figures are from birth. Once people have reached the age of 65, these numbers increase to 86 for women and 83 for men
- 45 per cent of Canadians who retire do so for reasons beyond their control, like their own health or the health of a family member or downsizing and layoffs at their workplace
- Many retirees return to the workforce in some capacity
- This generation of retirees has high expectations of their retirement

RETIREMENT SNAPSHOT

1. Average age at retirement is 61 (public sector), 64 (private sector), 66 (self-employed), and 63 generally. The trend is going up in age.
2. Shortages in the labour market and market downturns keep seniors working longer.
3. The number of single-person households is growing.
4. Over 75 per cent of retirees aged 64 to 75 own their own homes, but home ownership declines after age 75.
5. By the age of 65, 45 per cent of women are widows while 20 per cent of men are widowers. Men are more likely to remarry (widows outnumber widowers 4:1).
6. Private sector pensions are declining. Only about one-quarter of employees have employer pensions.
7. Many Canadians have no employer-sponsored pension plan, including the

self-employed, employees of small businesses, or employees of failed or failing businesses.

8. 58 per cent of Canadians are concerned about out-living their money – but right after retirement the figure is 29 per cent.
9. Retirement can last 25 to 35 years, often equal to the number of years spent in the workforce.
10. About 10 per cent who declared bankruptcy in 2014 were 65 or older.

REASONS FOR RETIREMENT

The most common reason for choosing retirement timing is a health issue. Others include feeling ready, hitting a certain age or pension factor, being laid off or let go, or getting an early retirement opportunity. It may be a combination of factors that just add up to the decision. A spouse may be retired or a family issue that requires more time commitments can take the focus off work. The final factor in the decision could be unwelcome changes at work or the completion of a project.

A planned, conscious decision makes for an easier adjustment than a spur-of-the-moment urge or a "take this job and shove it" moment. An early retirement offer or a sudden health problem can require some quick thinking. Early planning can make the difference in such cases between panic and a calm, clear choice.

WHAT PLANNING FOR RETIREMENT INVOLVES

- Developing an understanding of the meaning of retirement and the impact it will have on your life and lifestyle
- Acquiring the knowledge of what you can expect in later years
- Assessing realistically your personal resources such as health, finances, skills, interests, values, personal strengths, and social connectedness, as well as your ability to roll with the punches
- Considering various living arrangements and exploring leisure alternatives; redefining your identity

- Getting your financial and estate planning in place
- Putting new activities, interests, and social circles into your life before retirement to ease the transition

PUT YOUR TEAM TOGETHER

Here are some sources of expertise you may wish to consult; preferably, they'll be ones who listen to you and explain their services in a way you understand.

- Financial planner/advisor
- Tax planner/accountant
- Service Canada for CPP/QPP options, register online
- Employer for pension and benefits, timing factors
- Insurance broker
- Nutritionist
- Personal trainer
- Volunteer coordinator
- Already retired colleagues/friends
- Travel agent
- Family doctor
- Counsellor
- Spiritual and/or legal advisor

RETIREMENT: THE FINAL FRONTIER

Common expectations include:

- Begin/continue a fitness program

- Start a business
- Travel
- Enjoy leisure activities
- Do volunteer work
- Work around the house
- Take courses
- Find part-time employment
- Have fun
- Spend more time with family and friends
- Realize a goal, pursue a passion
- Spend more time on hobbies/interests

But then life can happen, including:

- Becoming a caregiver for a family member
- Returning to the workforce
- Experiencing illness or a chronic condition
- Facing divorce or separation
- Suffering financially in an economic downturn
- Grieving after a loss or a series of losses
- Experiencing loneliness, isolation, or depression
- Supporting an adult child and/or grandchildren
- Experiencing an identity crisis or depression
- Having an unexpected major expenditure

> There is more to life than increasing its speed.
>
> ~MAHATMA GANDHI

RETIREMENT PLANS AND EXPECTATIONS

TIMING

Figure out an approximate time for retirement; this will give you a target or goal to aim for in your planning. It could be an age or pension factor, or any combination of factors that makes sense to you. Then you have an idea of how many years, months, or weeks you have to get your plan in place.

FINANCES

Start to build your team of trusted advisors like a banker or financial planner; a lawyer or notary for wills and powers of attorney; an accountant, tax preparer, or whomever you feel you can trust and where you can get good advice and service.

Do an assessment of where you are by looking at your assets, present and anticipated cash flow, sources of income presently and in retirement, and the major expenses you want to take care of while still employed.

Figure out what kind of lifestyle you want in retirement and what that could cost. Lifestyle expectations and financial realities need to match.

HEALTH

Have a check up with your doctor and dentist. Use benefits you may have while employed to get what you need like glasses, dental work, or orthotics.

Start or continue a fitness regime that will take you into a long, healthy retirement.

LEISURE TIME/LIFESTYLE

Start sowing the garden of retirement now. Look around for what you want to do, with whom, and where that may be. Prepare the ground for what you will be doing with those extra hours. Figure out what you want to accomplish, or try out, for the period when you will have both time and energy. Imagine yourself retired and how you might spend your day during your active retirement.

> There are two things to aim at in life: first, to get what you want and, after that, to enjoy it. Only the wisest of mankind achieve the second.
>
> ~L.P. SMITH

RELATIONSHIPS

Now is the time to enrich your primary relationships and compare expectations and visions of retirement. Go and find the people who will be in your new life. You may want to join some new groups, start volunteering before retiring, become part of new social circles, and renew some friendships.

RESEARCH

Ask yourself some basic questions. Do you want to continue living where you are? Will you relocate or downsize? Do you want to work at something else full time or part time? Start a business? What will get you out of bed happy to experience the day? How will you reinvent yourself? Do you want to take courses, join interest groups, or reclaim an interest like art, music, sports, hiking, travelling, reading, dancing, or gardening?

ANTICIPATING PROBLEMS

What issues have you concerned? Take a look at your fears or hesitations about retirement. Finances, boredom, relationship changes, and loneliness are common ones. Take steps to reduce those fears by making changes prior to retiring. Design your retirement business card now.

> We are always getting ready to live, but not really living.
>
> ~RALPH WALDO EMERSON

YOUR RETIREMENT PLANNER			
RETIREMENT AGE	**SELF**	**SPOUSE**	
Target retirement age			
Number of working years remaining			
HOUSING	**YES/NO**	**YES/NO**	**NOT SURE**
Continue to live in present house			
Move to less expensive house			
Move to more expensive house			
Own more than one residence and will continue to do so			
Will acquire a second residence			
Will acquire more than one additional residence			
LIFESTYLE	**YES/NO**	**YES/NO**	**NOT SURE**
More time with family			
Travel			
Winters in the Sunbelt			
More sports activities			
Gardening			
Reading, watching TV			
Computers, Internet			
Hobbies			
Part-time work			
More active social life			
Start a business			
Volunteer/charitable work			
Improve health/fitness level			
Take courses			
Pursue new hobbies/interests			
Other (fill in your own priorities)			

BALANCING YOUR WHEEL OF LIFE

Retirement, as in every other stage of life, has many aspects; each one requires consideration and is affected by the choices you make. Think about what a typical week would look like for you in retirement.

Many who anticipate retirement are looking forward to a better balance in their lives. They want more time with family, for leisure and fun, friends, travel, reading, fitness, or just catching up on sleep. Figure out how life is out of balance and begin to rebalance where you can before you retire.

Find out if a phased retirement is possible by working part time, taking some time off, using your holiday time, or contracting back services. The most important immediate factor for positive adjustment has to do with conditions of leaving from work. Do your best to make it a pleasant exit. Try to get some time to start this rebalancing process as you ease into retirement.

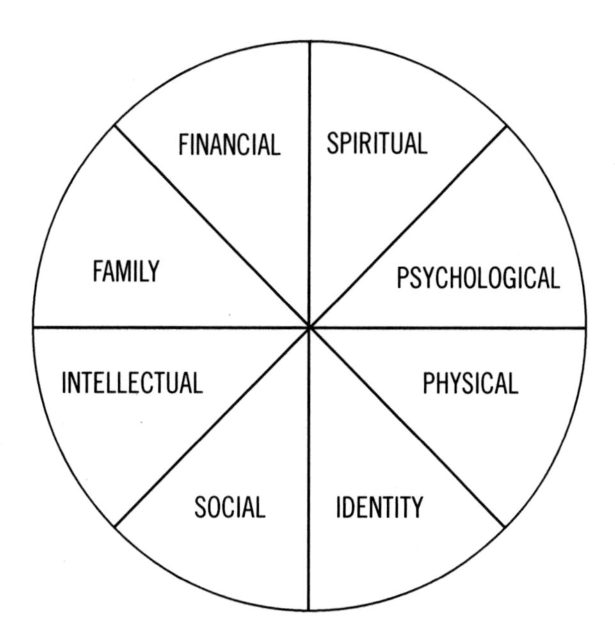

THREAT OR OPPORTUNITY?

Many people have difficulty with any kind of ending. In his book *Transitions,* William Bridges describes the first phase of a transition as beginning with an ending. Endings imply a sense of loss, of having to let go of what life was, yet endings are a normal part of each person's life and often serve a positive function. In order to begin something, we must let go and open the way for something new.

After the endings, the second phase is the neutral or "in between" zone, the period after something has ended but before something new has begun. This zone can be a time of reflection when you're able to think about what is really important to you and where your life is going. It can be an opportunity to make choices that will work for you. How can you make the choices that are best for you? You need a sound, internal reference point based on your core values and competencies.

THE ROLE OF THE JOB

As a retiree, you need to consider how needs that were met by employment will be met in retirement. Needs like:

- Income and benefits
- Belonging as a member of a meaningful group or groups
- The structure of day/week/year
- Socializing, social networking, and activities
- Opportunities for reward, advancement, accomplishment, status, satisfaction
- Opportunities for sharing, getting feedback, affirmation, and encouragement
- Setting and realizing goals
- A sense of identity, worth, and meaning
- A sense of contributing, being useful, and being productive
- A sense of being challenged to learn and achieve personal growth

> One of the symptoms of an approaching nervous breakdown is the belief that one's work is terribly important.
>
> ~BERTRAND RUSSELL

THE ROLE OF THE JOB (continued)

Consider what you will miss about your job, both negative and positive.

POSITIVE	**NEGATIVE**
Time structure	Time consuming
Sense of purpose	Energy consuming
Sense of belonging	Going through the motions
Friends/social activities	Restricts new opportunities/activities
Income/benefits	High stress levels
Respect/status/self-worth	Challenging relationships

Few people welcome change, especially if they are reasonably comfortable and unsure of exactly what the results will be. Someone once said, "No one likes change except a wet baby."

Making changes can be both exhilarating and anxiety provoking. You cannot stop the changes but you can decide how you will respond to change. The word "crisis" when written in Chinese has two characters: one represents danger; the other represents opportunity.

Change can be dangerous for you when you resist it; most of your energy will go into maintaining the status quo. Instead, use change to your advantage by seeing it as a source of opportunity rather than a threat. As you begin to see the changes as opportunities, you can decide which are best for you and how to take advantage of them. By actively deciding, you will gain more control over the way you respond. Remember, retirement is a process, not an event.

EMPLOYERS AND RETIREMENT PLANNING

According to a survey done in the fall of 2015, about 55 per cent of employers provide information on an internal or service provider's website or provide some tools for employees to explore retirement readiness. This is a very minimal, self-guided preparation.

About 48 per cent offer group financial planning or educational sessions that deal with finances only.

About 19 per cent have individual retirement-planning and educational sessions available to employees. Take advantage of these.

Only 11 per cent provide group sessions that deal with the psychological transition to retirement.

Finally, 27 per cent provide nothing at all.

Proper retirement preparation would consist of financial, psychological, and lifestyle preparation sessions. A full program would make succession smooth, allow for training of a replacement person, lessen any anxiety of pre-retirees, and make personal planning easier. Phased retirement options can be useful for both employer and employee, but only about 6 per cent of employers in the survey reported ease-out or flexible options. These options may be available on a personal request basis, though.

With over 16 per cent of the Canadian population over age 65 and rising fast, employers need to find ways to keep older workers by providing flexible work hours, for example.

MOURNING THE LOSS OF YOUR CAREER

Mourning the loss of your career can take you through these stages of grief:

1. Denial
2. Anger
3. Bargaining
4. Depression
5. Acceptance

Life situation transitions can trigger the same mourning process:

- Caring for a parent
- Having a parent, family member, or friend die
- Losing a job
- Getting a divorce
- Last child moving out
- Surviving an illness
- Losing someone close to you to relocation or illness

COMMON FEARS

- Poor health
- Isolation
- Boredom
- Loss of status
- Relationship issues
- Sense of loss/grief
- Financial problems
- Lack of meaning, engagement
- Expectations for care of others
- Declining health and independence

PERSONAL FANTASIES

- Sleeping in
- Travelling whenever
- Socializing
- Reading and/or pursuing hobbies
- Working on your house
- Setting up a work space at home
- Spending more time with family
- Taking courses you're interested in
- Volunteering
- Freedom to structure your time

List your fears about retirement:

- ____________________
- ____________________
- ____________________

List your fantasies:

- ____________________
- ____________________
- ____________________

LOOK BEFORE YOU LEAP

Retirement is not just struggling over the finish line of the work marathon. Work is more than just a paycheque; retirement is more than endless vacation time.

- Be aware that you do give up more than a paycheque when you retire. Your role, position, routines, companionship, and sense of self-worth are just a few of the aspects of your life that will change as part of retirement
- The honeymoon period lasts six months to two years, and then you realize that retirement may not be full-time travel and leisure

- An early retirement package is offered, your spouse is pressuring you, your new boss is an SOB, your last holiday was really fun, you are passed over for an advancement – these are only a few examples of poor reasons to retire. Do your own planning, including the *timing* of your retirement
- Be careful of relocating immediately
- Consider your choices to avoid boredom, shock, and loneliness
- Negotiate roles, time, and territory with your spouse
- Try living on 70 per cent of your income now
- The key is having a plan; it won't prevent the uncertainties of retirement from happening but can help you adjust accordingly and reduce stress as you adapt the plan to the circumstances

WHO'S IN CHARGE?

Retirement can give you more time with less stress, a time to explore what you wish, a time to bring balance to your life, a time to be who you really are.

No more rush hour, alarm clocks, working through lunch, deadlines, performance appraisals, and restricted vacation time. More naps, winters in a warm place, breakfast with a friend every Wednesday – you're in charge. It's your time. What are you looking forward to?

> If you love what you do, you will never work a day in your life.
>
> ~CHINESE PROVERB

TO RETIRE OR NOT TO RETIRE

Some people enjoy their work, their business, and their careers and positions so much, they choose not to retire. Some people feel they can't afford to retire. Some can't imagine what they would do in retirement. Farmers, artists, the self-employed, and professionals often delay retirement, men more than women. Health is often the deciding factor. This may be a spouse or family member's health.

Ask yourself whether you are retiring *from* something or *to* something or *both*.

The concept of retirement is evolving and being challenged by the Boomer generation. Many see this time period as a continuous series of transitions rather than one major change. Flexibility is the key as government and employers build in more opportunities for choice and continued contribution. Boomers are active, relatively healthy, and well educated and are an enormous resource of human capital.

Phased retirement or downshifting may be a good option. Some employers are designing their own plans for reducing their own time on the job – as well as designing similar plans for their employees. Canada has more people over age 65 than under age 15. With an aging population, governments are facing hard choices about health care, pharmacare, housing, and social supports for seniors. Fewer taxpayers support more and more dependents. Funding for Old Age Security pensions and the Guaranteed Income Supplement, health care, and a range of services are then tested to their limits.

The biggest advantages to retirement, according to a survey of retirees, are:

- Reduced stress
- A better life balance
- Flexibility of vacations
- Having choices about how time is spent

The number of 65-plus workers staying in the workforce is up 140 per cent. Many are still working in some capacity for income, meaningful contribution, physical activity, social connections, and mental stimulation. Women are also continuing to stay in the workforce. Many also want flexible hours, short-term projects, extended health-care benefits, and extra vacation time. About 60 per cent of employed seniors are self-employed.

Many seniors continue working, start a business, and find means to add income to maintain lifestyle. In fact, 30 per cent of new businesses are started by those over 50 years of age. Seniors are getting creative with means to increase income.

PHASED RETIREMENT

The federal budget of March 2007 brought in phased retirement. This allows employees with a defined benefit pension plan to draw down pension benefits while continuing to work. A serious labour shortage, an aging workforce, and the Baby Boomer silver tsunami are creating a demographic nightmare. Health-care and skilled labour shortages are real problems.

Phased retirement allows reduced work time without pension penalties and allows retirees to ease out of their workplaces more gradually. Phased retirement could take the form of a gradual reduction in hours or days, before full retirement, or post-retirement part-time work for pensioners at their previous place of employment. A phased approach helps employees avoid the shock of working full out and stopping abruptly at retirement. It becomes a glide rather than an abrupt stop.

RETIREMENT SHOCK

Retirement is a major life transition that can result in disorientation, depression, a loss of identity, physical illness, and mental anguish. Mariella Vigneux of Crabapple Coaching works with pre-and post-retirees and emphasizes lifestyle planning. She describes the "cauldron of emotions" bubbling up as "half terror and half enthusiasm and excitement." She warns of the downsides of not managing the transition well including depression, addiction, and inactivity.

> People who are serious write down their retirement goals. Putting plans in writing lets you identify where you are, where you want to go, and what you must do to get there.
>
> ~PAUL MERRIMAN, FINANCIAL ADVISOR

1. A loss of purpose may mean experiencing a negative sense of self-worth. Who am I now? How am I valuable?
2. The loss of structure and routine may create confusion and a sense of disorientation as one way of life has ended and another has not begun. It is Monday morning and what do I do after my coffee and newspaper?
3. A health crisis or a pink slip can usher in an unexpected retirement with a barrage of negative emotions overwhelming the new retiree. A crisis is no way to start retirement.
4. Some retirees go through the same stages of grief as if someone close to them died. This emotional roller coaster and the resulting behaviours can be confounding to family and friends. This, in turn, may lead to further conflict or isolation.
5. Some are exhausted or burned out at the outset of retirement, even blaming retirement for how they feel rather than taking time to recover. One person in my class blamed retirement, rather than burnout from his high-pressure job, for his illness.
6. Some experience a kind of withdrawal as an addict might have including mental and physical symptoms. It is a total lifestyle sudden change for many.
7. Couples can have trouble adjusting. Many are not on the same page. Nora Hall has written a book called *Surviving Your Husband's Retirement* and does workshops to help couples communicate and cope.
8. Lack of planning, poor time management, isolation, boredom, a lack of hobbies or interests, lack of physical and intellectual stimulation can all contribute to retirement shock. This can lead to serial retirements as unprepared retirees struggle with adjustments.
9. Wile E. Coyote Syndrome is what I call the experience of folks who rush to the finish line of their careers, nose to the grindstone the whole way. They have done little or no preparation and find themselves hanging over the canyon of nothing to do in retirement still spinning their wheels before they plunge into that canyon like Wile E. did so often in his pursuit of the Road Runner.

> I retired but it may have been too soon. I think I just needed a rest, some time off, and then go back to the job. I really miss it now.
>
> ~RECENT RETIREE

GETTING STARTED ✓ CHECKLIST

- ❑ I have talked to my family about my plans
- ❑ I have a good idea of my timing for retirement
- ❑ I will take advantage of employer preparation options
- ❑ I will take steps to prevent retirement shock
- ❑ I am considering a phasing out or reduction in hours at work
- ❑ I am considering a new position at work
- ❑ I have planned my retirement celebration
- ❑ I have plans for my retirement honeymoon
- ❑ I will work full or part time after retirement
- ❑ I plan to coach, mentor, or volunteer
- ❑ I plan to be a consultant, advisor, or board member
- ❑ I plan to work/volunteer overseas
- ❑ I plan to start my own business
- ❑ I have considered my need for engaging, meaningful activity
- ❑ I have started to shift attention from work
- ❑ I have started some new routines and activities
- ❑ I have connected with new social groups
- ❑ I am continuing or starting a fitness regime
- ❑ I am considering how to better balance my life

Section Two

Finances

FINANCIAL TIPS AND FACTS

The ideal is ... 50 to 70 per cent of your current income coming in and sustained during the length of your retirement to maintain your existing standard of living. But consider this: Were you ideally ready when you bought a house, had children, bought a new car? We often think there is never enough. We often lack the ideal means to deal with various situations but cope well enough all the same.

Usual sources of retirement income include:

- Old Age Security (OAS) and Canada Pension Plan (CPP/QPP) – both are indexed to inflation
- Guaranteed Income Supplement (GIS) are for lower-income seniors
- Employer pension plans
- Investments – Registered Retirement Savings Plan (RRSP), real estate, non-registered funds
- Inheritance
- Continued employment
- Tax Free Savings Account (TFSA)
- Rental income

FINANCIAL PLANNING

To become your own financial planner, find out about Registered Retirement Income Funds (RRIFs), annuities, Treasury Bills, Guaranteed Investment Certificates (GICs), Canada Savings Bonds, Money Market Funds, equities, pay-yourself-first options, dollar-cost averaging, diversified portfolio, bonds, taxation rates, estate planning, reverse mortgages, clawbacks, and timing options for CPP/QPP. Or, carefully choose a financial planner you trust to help you with all of these. You may wish to pay for independent advice.

- Research your employer pension thoroughly including survivorship
- Thoroughly investigate your options for the timing of your retirement with vacation time, sick leave, and extended benefits in mind
- Find out designations and fee structures of financial planners and advisors. Understand the basics of what you are invested in
- Look at options for benefit rollovers or insurance coverage for health and alternate health care
- Confer with your accountant about tax planning and implications of retirement
- Spend less – sort out needs versus wants
- Insurance: How much of what types do you need? Comparison-shop
- Look for long-term disability, critical illness, and long-term-care insurance
- Get estate planning, wills, powers of attorney, and living wills or health directives completed with a trusted legal advisor
- Estimate how long your savings may need to last
- Assess your housing needs and options
- Use your equity to your advantage to borrow, invest, or renovate, being aware of the debt hole risk
- Consider the effects of inflation
- Keep an emergency fund. Maintain some liquidity
- Boost your earnings (e.g., through part-time work, rental income)
- Car costs are about $10,500 per year, per car – this includes the cost of gas, insurance, and repairs (use the CAA Driving Costs Calculator to assess operating costs for your vehicle)
- Average inheritance in Canada is just under $100,000
- Women have lower earned income and savings than men on average – but live longer
- Make a charitable giving or legacy plan

GETTING PREPARED

- Have a plan/series of goals (e.g., pay off credit cards, mortgage, car, save for retirement, cut spending)
- Pay yourself first with automatic pay deductions to savings/investments
- Know the Tax Free Savings Account withdrawal and contribution rules
- Keep investments simple and easy to understand but appropriate to your situation and your comfort level with risk
- Keep some liquid assets so you have money available when you need it
- Know the costs of your investments
- Be careful of risky investments including some real estate schemes, get-rich-quick short cuts, and advertising promises. If it sounds too good to be true, it just may be
- Know your "burn factor" or "latte losses"
- Check your credit rating. You may need to reduce your number of credit cards
- Investment portfolios carry risks and costs. Consider liquidity (penalty-free available cash), tax implications, fee structures, reasonable return rates
- Figure out your assets, net worth, expenses, and cash flow
- Estimate your financial requirements and your income from various sources at retirement
- Focus on long-term growth and performance rather than the investment or financial flavour of the month
- Get out of debt starting with high-interest credit cards as about 40 per cent of Canadians have ugly credit card debt

USING RETIREMENT CALCULATORS

These calculators (available on various websites) provide an interesting exercise for speculation; however, too many unknowns creep in, like inflation rates, rates of return on investments, longevity, the value of your assets going forward, and surprises life may bring. These cannot be factored in reliably. Retirement calculators help get you thinking but should not be relied on as an action plan. Try the Canadian Retirement Income Calculator.

TIMING IS EVERYTHING

- For every year early you retire, you lose a year of potential savings, a year of growth in savings and investments – and gain a year of retirement expenses
- Longevity is a key factor to consider. According to Stats Canada, a 65-year-old man can expect to live to 83 and a woman to 86; these are averages, remember – some people are retired for 35-plus years
- The majority of retirees return to some form of paid employment. The income this provides can be the equivalent of what you would receive from a $500,000 retirement portfolio. At a 4 per cent pay-out rate, that would be $20,000 – the amount a part-time job could generate, for example

You can collect CPP/QPP at age 60. The longer you delay, the more you collect. You need to apply about six months before your first cheque. Service Canada can give you estimates for what your pension will be depending on when you collect it – age 60, 62, 65, for example.

The timing of retirement may be influenced by sick leave, holiday time, leave of absence, workload, health of retiree, or end of a project or contract. June is the most common month to retire. Make sure you have written the last chapter of your career epic.

CANADA PENSION PLAN REVISITED

The newest version of the Canada Pension Plan is phased in with a number of changes in place. Contributions increase from 4.95 per cent of salary to 5.95 per cent. The salary cap was $54,900 and goes up to $82,700 when fully realized in 2025.

Bear in mind that few actually receive the maximum annual payment. The CPP is designed to replace only a portion of working income. The amount received is based on work history and the amount paid into the plan over a lifetime of working. In 2016, the average payout monthly was $664.57 while the maximum was $1092.50 or $13,110 annually. That maximum goes up by $4,400 per year for those earning $55,000 a year. It goes to $19,900 for those earning $82,700 or more.

A tax break is built in for employees' contributions. The lack of employer pensions got the provinces to buy into a revised CPP. It is a money-for-life program that will benefit those starting their working lives at present and in the future. Those retiring in the next few decades will have very little benefit from these changes if any at all. For example, someone retiring in 2030 will have ten years of extra contributions. It is a pension for everyone and is secure compared with many other income sources.

INFLATION BITES!

At 3 per cent inflation, $3,000 a month in expenses will require $3,477.83 in five years to cover those expenses and $4,013.77 in ten years. Goods and services will probably continue to increase in price, as well. For example, if your estimated after-tax retirement income need is $50,000, a 2 per cent inflation rate means you will need over $90,000 in 30 years.

At a 2 per cent rate of inflation, $1,000, 20 years from now, will be worth the equivalent of $667 in today's dollars, which is a 33 per cent reduction. At 3 per cent, it will be a 45 per cent reduction. Inflation rates can vary widely from a low of 1 per cent to a high of 10 per cent.

Let's say you spend $600 per month on groceries. With an estimated inflation rate of 3 per cent per year, you'll be paying $695.56 in five years and $806.35 in ten years in today's dollars. It is important to plan for increased costs of services like health care.

GET YOUR FINANCIAL PICTURE IN FOCUS

- Figure out your present asset situation
- Calculate your net worth
- Sort out your cash flow – what is coming in and what is going out for expenses
- Project your retirement income and costs
- If there is a negative gap between money coming in and money going out, you know what you will need from other income sources or how much you need to cut back as you adjust your lifestyle

OWNERSHIP OF ASSETS

DESCRIPTION	ME	SPOUSE	CO-OWNERSHIP	OTHER
Bank accounts: - savings - chequing				
Investments: -certificates -stocks -bonds -mutual funds -TFSAs				
Real estate: - principal residence - other residences or properties				
Personal assets: - automobile(s) - boat(s) - furniture - other				
Insurance: - beneficiary				
Pension plan: - beneficiary - survivor				
Other:				

People spend money they haven't earned, to buy things they don't want, to impress people they don't like.

~WILL ROGERS

YOUR NET WORTH

ASSETS		**LIABILITIES**	
Bank accounts:	$	**Mortgage:**	$
Investments: - cash, bonds, GICs - interest bearing - equities, TFSA	 $ $ $	**Outstanding loans:**	 $ $ $
Real estate:	$	**Credit Cards:**	$
Other assets: - personal property - pension - cash surrender value of insurance	 $ $ $	**Accrued income** **taxes on investments:**	 $ $ $ $
Registered assets: - RRSP - pension plan - deferred profit sharing - RRIF	 $ $ $ $	**Others:**	 $ $ $ $ $
Vehicles: - book value	 $		
TOTAL ASSETS:	$	**TOTAL LIABILITIES**	$

NET WORTH: Total (Assets): $ ______________ – Total (Liabilities): $ ______________

= Net Worth: $ ______________

YOUR INCOME AND EXPENSE STATEMENT

SUMMARY OF REVENUES	MONTHLY	YEARLY
Income:		
- Net income	______	______
- Investment income	______	______
(interest, dividends, capital gains)	______	______
- Spouse's income	______	______
- Net pension income	______	______
- Other sources	______	______
TOTAL	$______	$______

SUMMARY OF EXPENSES	MONTHLY	YEARLY
Expenses:		
- Mortgage/rent	______	______
- Property taxes	______	______
- Maintenance and repairs	______	______
- Utilities: electric	______	______
heating	______	______
water & sewer	______	______
- Telephone	______	______
- Television	______	______
- Internet	______	______
- Food	______	______
- Insurance	______	______
- Credit cards	______	______
- Education	______	______
- Entertainment	______	______
- Donations	______	______
- Fitness	______	______
- Professional services	______	______
- Personal care	______	______
TOTAL	$______	$______

SUMMARY OF EXPENSES, *CONTINUED*	MONTHLY	YEARLY
- Medical and dental		
- Vacations	________	________
- Loan payments	________	________
- Transportation: fuel	________	________
insurance	________	________
licence fees	________	________
parking	________	________
maintenance	________	________
- Clothing	________	________
- Gifts	________	________
- Property maintenance	________	________
- Income tax	________	________
- Other a) ________	________	________
b) ________	________	________
c) ________	________	________
TOTAL	$________	$________
SURPLUS/DEFICIT:	$________	

Where costs could be reduced:

____

____

____

How income could be increased:

____

____

____

SO HOW MUCH DO I NEED, ANYWAY?

The best answer to that is it depends on a number of factors from how long you live to lifestyle choices to health-care costs or any number of surprises that life has in store. Too many put off planning as if they do not want to know or are afraid to take a hard look at their finances. If savings and debt reduction slide, time will eventually run out, leaving you scrambling. Denial is the wrong approach here. Get proactive.

A McMaster University study claims that a no-frills retirement may not require much more than government transfers like Old Age Security, the Guaranteed Income Supplement, and the Canada Pension Plan. A frugal lifestyle and paid-off debts help make this more palatable.

The average senior couple spends between $40,000 and $70,000 annually. This requires some supplementing from other sources like inheritance, employer pensions, rental income, wages, investments, and savings.

The deluxe retirement requires higher income in retirement from various sources.

To get an idea of your situation, get your CPP Statement of Contributions from Service Canada, your pension information from your employer if relevant, your investment statement or other savings and plug them into the Canadian Retirement Income Calculator and see where you are at with retirement income.

Dr. Michael Wolfson, who was the assistant chief statistician for Statistics Canada, warns that about half of middle-income Canadians can expect a 25 per cent drop in income once they finish work. An RBC poll found that many people were carrying mortgage debt, lines of credit, and consumer debt including credit cards into retirement counting on low interest rates to continue. A Manulife study found that six of ten people worried about money for retirement, and no wonder! Try living on 70-75 per cent of your income now to get the idea of what that could be like.

SOURCES OF INCOME

- Government transfers include the Old Age Security (OAS), which you qualify for if you have lived in Canada 40 years after the age of 18 and a partial payment if over ten years. It is worth about $7,000 annually but is indexed quarterly. It is clawed back in taxes after a certain level of income. Take a look at the Canada Revenue website for details

- The Guaranteed Income Supplement (GIS) goes to about three in ten retirees and is for those with low income. It is triggered by a low tax return or by your tax preparer who will advise you to apply for it. This is what makes our senior poverty statistics look so much better than our neighbours' to the south who have about a 25 per cent senior poverty rate. Those most at risk are single women, aboriginal and immigrant seniors, and those who are disabled

- The Canada Pension Plan is paid monthly, is indexed annually, and depends on your contributions while working, your age at application, and how much time you were out of the workforce. Few Canadians get the maximum. Some take a reduced pension before age 65 while others wait until after 65 for more money. There is a survivor portion for a spouse or children of the deceased. Contact Service Canada for more information

- Employer Sponsored Pension Plans. Over 6.2 million Canadians or about 38 per cent of the workforce are members of pension plans from their employers. The public sector is just over half of these employees. These plans are being downgraded regularly. The defined benefit pension is associated with education, public service, and some larger workplaces. Many have been converted to defined contribution where the risk is that of the employee rather than the employer
- Other income would come from Tax Free Saving Accounts, other savings, investments, rental income, wages, sale of goods or properties, annuities, insurance payments, or inheritances
- Registered Retirement Savings Plans. In 2014, just under 6 million tax filers contributed to an RRSP. The median amount was $3,000. That means that only about 23 per cent of tax filers made a contribution. The limit of contribution is based on 18 per cent of the previous year's income less any pension adjustments and unused room carried forward. Check your Statement of Adjustments or with your tax preparer for your information

FINANCIAL CONSIDERATIONS

LONGEVITY RISK

None of us has a crystal ball to know the hour of our demise. About 45 per cent of Canadians say they are concerned that they will outlive their assets. All we have is insight into our genetic risks and lifestyle risks, as well as actuarial information. Some of those risk factors are smoking, excessive alcohol, poor diet, a sedentary lifestyle, stress, and social isolation.

Canadian men who make it to 65 live on average 17 more years, with 8 of those in good health. Women live another 19.7 years, with 11.3 of those in good health. In fact, women have a 53.2 per cent chance of making it to age 90 while men have an 18.3 per cent chance. This means provisions need to be made for a thirty-plus-year retirement, particularly for women.

LIFESTYLE

Lifestyle and incomes need to match to avoid going into debt. Most people make the adjustment just fine. Other do struggle and have to get creative.

Lifestyle adjustments can include continuing to work in some capacity, accepting a lower standard of living, downsizing to a less expensive home, or borrowing against equity as a last resort. The 65-plus crowd is going into debt faster than any other cohort, and delinquency rates are rising. Bankruptcies by those over 65 have gone up 20.5 per cent since 2010. According to Statistics Canada, 40 per cent of retirees carry some form of debt with housing and transportation the biggest costs. The old rule of pay off debts before retiring still holds in theory but not so much in practice.

FATE AND OTHER FACTORS

One factor is timing of retirement. The earlier you retire, the more money you need to finance that retirement. You stop contributing to CPP, lose employment income and benefits that need to be replaced, and have more time to shop, travel, and spend. Figure out your retirement price tag early.

Women tend to retire earlier than men and live longer. They also are more likely to work in the public sector or the health or educational fields or be in other professions where they may have good employer pensions. People who retire latest are the self-employed, particularly farmers, some professionals, and those in the creative arts. They tell me they are on the Freedom 85 plan.

Another major factor is health. It is the snake in the woodpile here. According to a Sun Life Canadian Health Index, of those who retire early, 41 per cent said health was the reason. For those who experience a significant health event, 45 per cent ended up retiring and 26 per cent of those experienced some financial hardship. Options to go back to work exist for those who are healthy. Those who retire early are most likely to go back to some form of employment as long as they have the health to do so. Also, health-care costs start to rise around age 75 and can be a challenge for the unprepared.

About half of women and 40 per cent of men will go into long-term care, which can be very costly in a private institution or somewhat less in a public one. Care may involve bathing, dressing, toileting, transferring, and feeding as a result of a physical condition or a cognitive impairment. Costs can be between $35,000 and $100,000 per year depending on the place and type of care required.

A report from the Ontario Securities Commission says nearly six of ten older

Canadians have experienced a major life event that disrupted their financial plans. For those over 75, that event was usually health related.

FINANCIAL SHIFTS AT RETIREMENT

WHAT GOES DOWN:	EI
↓	CPP/QPP contributions
... and POSSIBLY:	Pension/RRSP contributions
→	Disability insurance premiums
	Clothing, parking, lunches
	Transportation/commuting costs
	Income tax
	Savings
	Car insurance
	Gifts, social fund costs
	Union dues, professional memberships
WHAT GOES UP:	Benefits
↑	– health-care costs
	– dental coverage and care
	– prescriptions
	Inflation effect
	Leisure activities/vacations/travel/recreation
	Personal care, especially with chronic illness or injury
	In the honeymoon stage of retirement, travel is the biggest expenditure

Many retirees expect monthly expenses to drop at retirement, but 50 per cent found they stay about the same or actually go up.

NOW WHAT?

- Simplify/toss and sort/recycle/repurpose/downsize
- Biggest costs – housing and transportation
- Plan ahead for independent living at each stage of retirement

- Get your spreadsheets ready to show your accountant, tax preparer, or financial planner
- Know your CPP/QPP options; your pension details
- Know your benefits and insurance options
- Research your province's services for seniors as some allow property taxes to be deferred, and others have prescription drug programs

Try living on 70 per cent of your income, and put the other 30 per cent into your RRSP, mortgage repayment, upgrading your vehicle, or savings. See how you fare on what could be your retirement income.

Before retiring, you may want to replace your car, roof, windows, appliances, or furnace and get all your dental work done to help minimize any major cost surprises that could hit you in your more financially vulnerable early retirement years.

It may be time to begin guerrilla frugality while still employed: cutting costs, saving and investing, downsizing, and planning your taxes.

INCOME REALITIES

1. Defined benefit pensions have been declining, especially in the private sector. Some have been changed to defined contribution pensions, while others have disappeared entirely. As Neil McDonald of CBC News described the situation: "Defined benefit pension plans are rapidly being fossilized, replaced by defined contribution plans which is an HR department euphemism for bank accounts."
2. The majority of Canadian workers do not have an employer pension plan.
3. According to Michael Wolfson and a study he authored for Research on Public Policy, half of Canadian middle-income earners will see at least a 25 per cent drop in their disposable incomes at retirement. The CPP reform between 2019 and 2025 will not change this picture very much at all for a few decades.
4. Many Baby Boomers retire in debt and struggle with repayment.
5. The director of the International Centre for Pension Management at the Rotman School of Management argues that families with annual incomes of $30,000 to $100,000 are at the greatest risk.

6. Savings levels have dropped while debt levels continue to climb. According to the *Globe and Mail* of March 2016, the ratio of household credit-market debt to disposable income went up to just over $1.65 per dollar. Statistics Canada in 2012 said that 42.5 per cent of people 65 and older are still in debt.

7. Benefits Canada says that 59 per cent of recent retirees are concerned that their savings are not adequate.

8. According to the federal Office of the Superintendent of Bankruptcy, 10 per cent of those who declared bankruptcy in 2014 were 65 years of age or older. That rate is up 20.5 per cent from 2010.

9. Pension contribution rates differ from one pension to another. The Ontario Teachers' Pension Plan has contribution rates from 11.5 to 13.1 per cent of income, for example. Those without pensions need to be saving and investing at this rate or higher from their incomes. Susan Eng of the Canadian Association of Retired Persons suggests 18-20 per cent savings rate to achieve a 70 per cent replacement rate. Many do just fine on 50 per cent replacement with low overhead and minimal or no debt.

10. The uncertainty of income in the switch from defined benefit to defined contribution pension keeps employees working longer.

11. The number of participants in the labour force who are 55-plus continues to rise.

WHAT YOU NEED TO KNOW

- 84 per cent of public service workers have pensions
- 78 per cent of those plans are secure defined benefit pensions pegged to inflation
- 25 per cent of private sector workers have a pension plan
- 16 per cent of these plans are secure defined benefit pensions

> Money may be the husk of many things, but not the kernel. It brings you food, but not appetite; medicine, but not health; acquaintances, but not friends; servants, but not loyalty; days of joy, but not peace or happiness.
>
> ~HENRIK IBSEN

- 11 million workers, or 60 per cent of Canada's workers, have no employer pension at all
- Eight million, or 45 per cent, have no employer pensions or Registered Retirement Savings Plans (RRSPs)
- Ask your financial advisor if your portfolio is positioned for a comfortable retirement, if it is balanced between safety and growth, and if it needs adjustment

FIGURE OUT YOUR FUTURE INCOME

1. Find out what the survivorship benefits are in both public and private pensions.
2. CPP/QPP rates are adjusted annually while the OAS and GIS are adjusted quarterly. These are the public pensions (hrsdc.gc.ca).
3. Private pensions are defined benefit (DB) pensions or defined contribution (DC) pensions, or a combination. The defined benefit pension provides a regular income stream calculated according to a predetermined formula. The employer carries the market risk, hence these are declining as an option by employers. Most are indexed to inflation and adjusted annually. The defined contribution pension defines the annual contribution by the employer and, possibly, the employee. The size of the pension depends on the amount of money accumulated through contributions and earnings of the plan. The market risk is the employee's in this case.
4. Some are deferred profit sharing plans (DPSP), where a portion of company profits are paid into a fund for employees.
5. Find out the payout schedule. For example, it may be paid at the end of each month.
6. Find out: if there is an eligibility period to belong to the plan; the nature of your contributions; the timing of when the plan vests so that you are entitled to the employer's contributions; your ability to top up or pay back any withdrawals; the transferability or portability of the pension; provision of indexing; and the rules about survivorship.
7. Find out if the pension is integrated with CPP/QPP/OAS and what this means.
8. Take full advantage of RRSPs, if you do not have a defined benefit pension, and TFSAs.

PENSION ENVY

Fully indexed defined benefit pensions are considered to be the Cadillac of pension plans, but they are on the decline. Thirty years ago, 31 per cent of workers in the private sector were enrolled in these plans, but now it is only half that and falling. Public sector workers, teachers, and full-time nurses are examples of those with these pensions. The protection they offer from the effects of inflation makes them ideal for many.

CUSHIONING SURPRISES

Being prepared not scared for what life throws you is a challenge. Crap happens.

1. Asset splitting if a gray divorce happens can throw plans off dramatically.
2. A debilitating health crisis or disability can interrupt earnings and drain the coffers. By age 65, one-third of people will have a disability or chronic condition of some sort, and by 75, it is one-half. That can mean relocation or renovation costs, too.
3. Inflation does not retire and can eat up resources Pac Man like.
4. Boomerang adult children can show up on your doorstep, ask for a significant loan, or may suffer their own divorce or health setback.
5. Market downturns can drag your assets down significantly.
6. The fickle finger of fate can just point at you. Seniors made up 10 per cent of bankruptcies in 2014, and, in Ontario, seniors make up 35 per cent of food bank users.
7. A job loss can happen for various reasons.
8. The death of a spouse is profound in so many ways. 1.3 million women and 350,000 men are widowed annually in Canada. One in three over 65 live alone and one in two do so by the age of 80.

A gentleman explained to me that he was still working in his professional position in his 70s because he was supporting his ailing wife and his adult daughter and her three children. That had not been part of his retirement plan.

> Money is not everything but it does settle the nerves.
>
> ~IRISH SAYING

OPTIONS AND IDEAS

1. Couples counselling, negotiated arrangements, clear communication along the way, and understandings can make a positive difference in a relationship.
2. Disability or Critical Care insurance, good benefits, and a just-in-case savings account can mitigate health costs. A healthy lifestyle helps. Take the time to be healthy or you may have to take the time to be out of commission.
3. A proper financial plan takes inflation into account. The majority of Canadians do not have a written financial plan or planner. A good retirement plan includes both a financial plan and a lifestyle plan.
4. Cosign for a loan, offer a low-interest loan with a payback plan, give out the legacy early, but figure out how to help family members without risking your own well-being, if possible.
5. Diversify. Keep your eyes on the eggs in the baskets. Apply for public pensions like OAS when you qualify. Many do not.
6. Have a cushion of savings, assets, and options. A good social and family network helps, too.
7. Keep your skills up to date and your options open.
8. Plan for a possible death with insurance, an up-to-date will and estate planning, beneficiary designations, and a clear plan for financial security as one source of income is gone with the partner.
9. Play the What If game for possible downturns to see if you are prepared and protected. Play dead and see how your planning works out.
10. Work out your retirement price tag and your paycheques.

DELAYED RETIREMENT

Boomers make up about one-third of the workforce, and the generation just behind them is small. The 60-plus group make up one-third of new job gains since 2009. Over half of workers aged 55 to 64 are reemployed after retirement, men more than women. This group is putting more gold into the golden years by staying in the world of work. Terms like boomerang workers and boomerpreneurs reflect a new retiree reality.

Boomers are healthier and expect to live long lives. Many are still in debt, supporting family, and maintaining lifestyles, and mandatory retirement is no longer an issue. Many enjoy the work they do, find it rewarding, and feel too young to retire.

For some, retirement is a transition to a new form of working. They start businesses, work on contract or part time, or find a new position. Some have felt the sting of ageism as they are denied promotions or training, or are demoted and eased out or even tossed out. Some of them try to find or create another position.

Employers who want to keep older workers, particularly those in senior positions, need an engagement strategy. Some new policies need to happen if they want to keep people with valuable experience, knowledge, and skills. Employers motivated to make the most of the talent of older workers are offering phased retirement, job sharing, part-time positions, caretaking or medical leaves, and flexible hours, or are creating a retiree resource pool. Workplaces need to establish an inclusive culture with work from home opportunities, mentoring programs, contract back options, and other means of keeping and attracting valuable older employees.

Lisa Taylor and the Challenge Factory provide services for older workers seeking a new challenge, a more meaningful career, or another job opportunity. Lisa also advises employers about how to capitalize on their older workforce. Third Quarter, a non-profit organization, recruits older workers. In the United States, Marc Freedman has a site called Encore.org that invites people to unretirement, creating dynamic, engaged, and meaningful futures that can include paid employment.

Labour shortages loom as Boomers retire. Some may be encouraged to return to work. Many professionals will continue to work into their 80s, redefining the boundaries of what has been deemed possible, as Boomers have done historically.

THE AGE OF AGING

So many Boomers are concerned about outliving their assets and some for very good reason. Two-thirds of those who have lived over 65 are alive now. The 80-plus are a fast-growing demographic. Life expectancy is rising. It is not called the Silver Tsunami or Geezer Gusher for nothing.

Life is uncertain and unpredictable, but variables like genetic history, health status and lifestyle, gender, social class, and place of residence are relevant variables for lifespan.

Here are some statistical probabilities that can help someone decide whether or not to bet on an annuity as a pay for life option. If a female in Canada reaches the age of 65, she has a 14 per cent chance of reaching 95, while her male counterpart has a 5.5 per cent chance.

Doctors tell me that hip replacements for patients at age 95 are a reality. Meanwhile, eat your fruits and veggies, use sunscreen, get daily exercise, and stay engaged. We do not have longevity insurance yet. Some will be retired for a longer period than their working years. Planning for a 30-plus-year retirement requires some serious management.

Live long and hope to prosper!

PROTECT YOUR ESTATE

Here are some strategies for keeping wealth all in the family:

1. Look into setting up assets, such as buildings, cottages, or other non-primary-residence property, as trusts (family or testamentary, for example) or corporations, to minimize capital gains and other taxes as well as other costs that might otherwise come out of the estate.

2. Ensure that enough liquid assets such as cash, stocks, and bonds are available to pay taxes that might otherwise shrink the estate. Timing of insurance payouts may vary, making readily available cash preferable.

3. Look into investment vehicles that are especially estate friendly, such as insurance options like segregated funds. These come into play for the elderly in particular because they are expensive. Because they act as an insurance payout, they avoid probate.

4. Register assets in joint ownership, which is a simple way to transfer assets. Although useful for avoiding final taxes, there may be other tax and legal complications – an adult child's divorce or bankruptcy, for example. Create a separate account from your partner to avoid mingling everything that is owned and to protect inheritances and other assets from divorce, breakups, and lawsuits.

5. Gifting can be a simple solution, but do get expert advice about the best way to proceed.

6. Look into insurance options.

7. Attend estate-planning presentations.

8. The cost of a modest funeral is about $10,000; allow for this with your liquid assets or consider ABC (affordable burial and cremation).

9. Over 50 per cent of Canadians do not have an up-to-date will. Make one! Confer with your lawyer, accountant, and financial planner regarding the tax implications that come with your bequests. To test the will, check with your accountant to see what would happen in the event of your death. Play dead and see what happens. If there is a problem, go back to your lawyer to fix it.
10. Make sure you have a record of all your assets – including personal property, debts, your living will, your powers of attorney for personal care and property – readily available to your family and executor in case of accident, debilitating illness, or death. Photos of your possessions could also be included.
11. When you die, the government treats your assets as if everything had been sold just before your death. Some assets will be subject to capital gains taxes. Choosing favourite charities for bequests can offset taxes.
12. Fees (1.5 per cent) are charged on the inventory of final assets in your estate. Some insurance products avoid this as does joint ownership, which does carry some risk, as well.
13. Choose your executor(s) wisely as he/she/they arrange the funeral, review the will, file the final tax return, settle debts, and distribute assets to beneficiaries. Research changes to the executor role and liability.
14. Update your will regularly and as your situation changes. Check with your accountant and financial advisor, as well as your lawyer.

WHERE IS YOUR INFORMATION?

Make sure you have a safe, a safety deposit box, or a fireproof container to store your will, health directive, power of attorney, location of assets, and last wishes. Have copies with your lawyer, your executor(s), and/or a trusted person.

Include your SIN, passport or a copy of it, health card number, birth and marriage certificates, notice of divorce, and driver's licence number or copies.

> There is no more fatal blunderer than he who consumes the greater part of his life getting his living.
>
> ~HENRY DAVID

You may want to include a list of details about any pension plans, investment, debts, credit cards, club and other memberships, time share ownership, or philanthropic initiatives you have.

Figure out who will delete your online persona, as well.

CLIMB OUT OF THE DEBT HOLE

Canadians have been digging themselves into deeper and deeper debt holes. Mortgage debt has gone up 6.3 per cent while disposable income has gone up only 3 per cent. The ratio of household credit-market debt to disposable income is up to $1.65.4 per $1.00 of disposable income.

Interest rates at record lows make this possible without too much of a pinch. These historical lows may not last indefinitely. The strength of the Canadian dollar or lack of it against foreign currency can also cramp travel plans including for snowbirds fleeing winter.

The Parliamentary Budget office warns that Canadians have had the sharpest rise in debt in any G7 country since 1990. Rugs can be pulled out at any time by health issues, loss of income, the need to support a family member, or another major market downturn.

Canada's poverty rates for seniors dropped when the Guaranteed Income Supplement was introduced but are on the rise again.

About one-third of those who get OAS in Canada also receive the GIS.

Check out the Canadian Retirement Income Calculator at esdc.gc.ca for a look at sources of income and your situation.

WHAM BAM MONEY GONE SCAMS

Fraudsters often target the 80-plus group and also those 50 to 64 years old as they fit the "I am scared I won't have enough to retire" profile. These sophisticated profilers know how to push emotional buttons like fear and get personal information. The "deals" can look good, and many want to recoup losses from 2008-2009 market drops. The "marks" for these fraudsters are often male from this age group who are risk-takers, well off, and well educated. They are also likely to be embarrassed and not report fraud.

Officially, Canadians lost just over $61 million to scammers in 2015, but many do not report losses and so the actual amount is likely much higher.

TOP TEN SCAMS

1. Phishing emails or calls ask for a reply, a cheque, or personal identity information. They may claim to be from the bank or the CRA. Delete or hang up!
2. Online dating scams create a love interest, build a relationship, and then ask for personal information and money. Do not let your heartstrings be played.
3. You are a winner! These fake claims ask for a transfer fee in order to collect your windfall. Don't fall for it.
4. High-risk investments or get-rich schemes that are a once-in-a-lifetime opportunity may be too good to be true. It may be a pyramid scheme, or a gold mine in Labrador you will want to get in on fast. Or not. Do your due diligence.
5. Employment scams can include one where you receive a big cheque and are asked to deposit it and send some of the money back. Then the cheque bounces, and your money is long gone. Research the company or prize and the offer carefully.
6. Subscriptions you sign up for with your credit card may result in a large administration charge or a series of small ones you did not anticipate. Read the small print or avoid giving out credit card information altogether.
7. Smart scammers can create emails and websites that look really enticing. Thank twice before you click.
8. Websites like Craigslist and others can unwittingly host scammers. Face-to-face local deals are less risky. Be careful with how you are asked to pay.
9. If asked by a family member to bail them out of jail or pay legal fees or send money to get them home again from a trip, check with other family to see if they really are family.
10. Be on guard against anyone who will lend you money for an upfront fee.

Check with the Financial Consumer Agency of Canada and the Canadian Anti-Fraud Centre and report fraudulent activity.

FINANCIAL ABUSE OF SENIORS

Financial abuse is the second most frequent form of elder abuse in Canada. Caregivers, neighbours, family members, or other predators try to get a person to give them money or possessions or title to property. Sometimes, they take it outright.

According to Dr. Lynn McDonald of the National Initiative of the Care of the Elderly (NICE) at University of Toronto, this type of abuse affects at least 2.6 per cent of older Canadians.

Other forms of abuse include neglect and psychological, physical, and sexual abuse. Two stories in one newspaper illustrate this. In one, a 56-year-old son-in-law beat a 75-year-old woman to force her to sign a document that would forgive his debts to her. In the other, a 61-year-old son assaulted his mother putting her into intensive care. He had been taking money from her and was upset when she refused to give him more.

Patient-on-patient violence and abuse is also an issue in hospitals and nursing homes.

LIVING OUT OF COUNTRY

- Read *The Canadian Snowbird Guide* by Douglas Gray
- Rent accommodation first to check out the location
- Consider medical care, tax implications, safety issues, day-to-day living, housing costs, political stability, culture, climate, cost of living, the nature of the expat community, transportation, and life-long learning options
- Remember that property and personal possessions in various states of the United States are subject to state and federal death taxes
- Health care in Canada requires residency. Find out the rules
- Look into health insurance costs
- Spend time before making any purchase. Try it out
- Consider threats of hurricanes, tornadoes, earthquakes, local crime rates, local health problems, water and food security, and cultural and language barriers

YOUR HOME

- Real estate market values can be a significant part of family assets
- One-quarter of Canadians plan to use home equity for retirement income
- Trading down and downsizing can be a challenge, cost more, and take longer than expected. You can find a less expensive home and community and realize a profit on the sale of your home, but not everyone does
- Remember the impact of moving costs, real estate, legal fees, taxes, redecorating, and refurnishing
- Consider where your social connections and family members are located
- Consider a one-story, one-level home with trip-free flooring, space for a caregiver, night lights, and motion-activated lighting and faucets
- Check provincial tax rates and property taxes before you decide to move
- If your new home is a condo or land lease, check the fees involved
- Choosing a community may be based on your values – condo, townhouse, retirement community, winterized cottage, close to walking trails, skiing, golf, environmentally responsible community, vibrant arts community, offshore destination, mixed or seniors only, downtown, country, small town, good public transit, bike trails, hospital and medical facilities, climate, air and water quality, cost of living, public safety (whoseyourcity.com)
- You may want to get the feel of retirement before making major changes like selling your principal residence
- Your home is tax-free equity as your principal residence
- Clean out clutter, sort and toss, sell or give away unused items
- Pretend you're going to move even if you're not and get everything sorted out
- Read Lyndsay Green's *The Perfect Home for a Long Life*
- Find a roommate or housemate to share costs
- Golden Girls ads are becoming more popular

- Another factor in home decisions may be late-to-launch or boomerang adult children. According to the 2011 census, 42.3 per cent of those 20 to 29 years old are living in the parental home. Adult children may have their own homes but require financial support or bailouts. Slow economic growth has put many young people in financial straits
- The location of your family members, parents, adult children, and grandchildren may also be a factor in your decisions about housing 40 per cent of Boomers say they will move to smaller digs to reduce costs, allow carefree travel, and free up capital
- Bungalows, condos, and rental apartments are the most popular choices

AGING IN PLACE BY RENOVATION AND DESIGN

Boomers often think of themselves as super seniors or the forever young and, as a generation, they are healthier and longer-lived than past generations. Many want to stay in their homes and neighbourhoods. Some relocate but some renovate to get what they want.

If relocating, watch for, and if renovating, include, design aspects that will make aging in place safer and more pleasant

- Install grab bars in the most dangerous room in the house, the bathroom. Add higher toilets and a walk-in shower with a movable seat and a shower curtain
- Make doors extra wide to accommodate walkers, wheelchairs, canes, or other aids
- Have remote-controlled garage doors, window covers, and fans
- Install non-slip flooring that is easy on the knees
- Improve the lighting in all rooms, hallways, and entrances
- Eliminate stairs where possible or make sure sturdy railings are in place
- You may want room-to-room communications systems
- Use non-toxic, natural materials

> He worked like hell in the country so he could live in the city, where he worked like hell so he could live in the country.
>
> ~DON MARQUIS

- Put switches, thermostats, and electrical outlets in easily accessible locations, not too high or too low
- Use lever doorknobs or faucets
- Get rid of scatter mats and other trip and slip hazards
- Have an open floor plan
- Buy appliances and cabinets with easy open drawers
- Research universal design and use the resources already out there like CMHC's checklists and guides for independent living
- Hire the help that you need as you age rather than trying to do everything yourself. In Victoria, Canada's oldest with about 18 per cent seniors, I met a renovator who specializes in renovations to support disability and aging. He is busy!
- Downsizing companies have sprung up, as well, to help with moves
- Sometimes one layer of the sandwich generation also needs housing, and so adult children or their grandparents may be looking to share space
- Co-housing, shared housing, supportive, or cooperative housing may be alternatives, as well

SNOWBIRDING

Monthly rental in a warm climate need not be all that costly. In fact, some retirees find that three months away can cost about the same as a two-week luxury vacation. Property ownership is not necessary because many reasonably priced options are available, from house swaps to trailer rentals.

Many online sites open up possibilities for housing exchanges, overseas volunteering, teaching, or working on organic farms (WWOOFING), not to mention crewing on sailboats or dancing on cruise ships. Many retirees teach English as a second language, lead hikes or tours, or work in national parks or historic sites that may include housing. House sitting is another option. Health and travel insurance are musts.

If you are a cruise ship fan, look into health-care costs onboard and remember your health insurance.

FINANCIAL AND LEGAL DUCKS IN A ROW

Too many Canadians do not have an updated will. Here is a statistic that may get your attention: 100 per cent of us will die at some point!

Power of attorney for finances allows someone to pay your bills and taxes if you do not have the ability or capacity to do so.

Keep up to date on laws as they related to tax and estate planning. The role of an executor now is more complicated than many realize, for example. You may also find out about tax credits you are eligible for.

Consult your legal and financial advisors before making significant decisions about joint ownership, estate planning, capital gains, and named beneficiaries. Make sure your decisions are going to have the outcomes that you wish. You will not want to leave your family with a legal and administrative mess.

Find out what happens if you or a loved one loses capacity. Beware of undue influence that may be subtle or overt. Get your documentation in order sooner rather than later.

When it comes to family and the bank of Mom and Dad, figure out what is a gift and what is a loan. Have this in writing with particulars spelled out. In addition:

- Create appropriate trusts for disabled or vulnerable family members
- Have a personal directive or Advanced Health Care Directive in place
- Have a safe location for all documents that is accessible to those you choose
- Review and update your insurance coverage
- Protect yourself from fraud and scams
- Consider financial and taxation implications for extended trips outside of Canada

GETTING ADVICE

In addition to your investments, your advisor can tailor a plan to fit your needs and goals for:

Insurance – What you need and what you do not need.

Taxes – Planning, income splitting, reduction.

Estate planning – Tax-efficient way to get your assets to the people, charities, or institutions of your choice.

Coordination of services – Working with your team, including tax preparer/accountant, legal advisor, insurance provider.

WHAT ABOUT INSURANCE?

Like so many other answers, this one is also it depends. About 66 per cent of Canadians say health is a concern, but only 22 per cent have saved money, purchased insurance, or made provision for extra health-care costs.

Life Insurance

If spousal support or dependent children need support then life insurance can help with named beneficiaries taken care of in the event of a death. If this is not the case, perhaps it is not needed. If you do want it, get it before you are in poor health and either uninsurable or very expensive to insure.

The other reason for life insurance is estate preservation. Often there are substantial taxes owing on the final tax return. Life insurance, which pays out tax-free, can be used to mitigate this cost to allow full transfer of the estate.

Disability Insurance

This kind of insurance makes sense if you are still working and need insurance to pay bills if you cannot get your paycheque due to an illness or disability. It is insurance for your financial security in the face of a health issue during your working life. Employer-sponsored plans stop payments when you reach age 65.

Check with the FCAC for government information on living with a disability, as well as Employment and Social Development Canada.

Critical Illness Insurance

Many Canadians fear the implications of such a health crisis but do little to protect against one. If you are concerned about the financial implications of a health crisis, critical health insurance may settle the nerves. This provides a tax-free lump sum payment to deal with the financial aspects of a life-changing illness like cancer or heart problems. Treatment and recovery take time and cost money when you are unable to work. Drawing from your RRSP and savings may substantially interfere with retirement plans. Critical Illness insurance can cover costs and preserve savings.

Long-term Care Insurance

If 50 per cent of women and 40 per cent of men need long-term residential care at some point, you know how to play those odds. In addition, you may need home care, and this type of insurance can help cover those extra costs. In some cases, Disability or Critical Illness insurance may be converted to Long Term Care.

Home Insurance

With more seniors aging in place, the need for careful monitoring of home insurance comes up as those seniors may be away travelling or in hospital, respite, or rehabilitation facilities. These temporary absences can be a problem if homes are left vacant. Check the conditions for coverage as they may specify turning off the water or having a trusted person check the property every day. Make sure you know the renewal date and do not miss it.

Know whose name is on your policies and where they actually are located.

Disability

Employer-paid disability payments stop when a person becomes 65 years of age. Check with the FCAC for government information on living with a disability, as well as Employment and Social Development Canada. Read Ed Arbuckle's book *The Family Guide to Disability and Finances.*

Research these and other sites:

1. fpsccanada.org – Financial Planners Standards Council.
2. iafp.ca – Institute of Advanced Financial Planners ("Find a Planner" tool).
3. cfainstitute.org – Chartered Financial Analyst.
4. mfda.ca – Mutual Fund Dealers Association.
5. iiroc.ca – Investment Industry Organization of Canada (advisor report for background checks).
6. wheredoesallmymoneygo.com
7. retirehappy.ca
8. unretired.life

Find out:

- What training and designations the experts on your team hold, including their ongoing training

- How they are paid: for example, fee – flat or hourly; commission by percentage of assets; or as part of the mutual fund's management fees. You may pay for independent advice or pay no fee to someone who is paid based on what is sold to you
- What is included in the financial plan, the advisors' investment style or approach, and suggestions for further professional advice
- How long they have been in business, how many clients they have, their track record over a few years, and how they communicate with you as the client
- How the advisors keep you informed. You need to feel confident in your advisors. Clear communication and trust are key components in these as in any relationships

A WORD TO WOMEN ON RETIREMENT AND FINANCES

- Women are more likely to have broken career paths, non-standard work arrangements, and part-time work, and, on average, they earn 23 per cent less than men. The CPP is based on those lower wages. Women also tend to retire earlier than men, which, again, reduces their future incomes
- Women may be a bit more likely to have an employer pension but are less likely to be in a union
- Women aged 45 to 54 earn about $24,000 a year less than men. That fact and other considerations means women's savings are about 40 per cent less than men's, and they have fewer RRSPs and other investments. Those who do invest often choose very conservative options
- Nine out of ten women will be on their own and in charge of finances at some point. Some never marry or partner, others are separated or divorce, and others are widowed
- Only about one-third of women have a financial plan
- Ignorance is not bliss when it comes to finances. Women often give over control of their money to others including bad advisors or ill-informed, impatient or even greedy heirs. This plays out with figures like 75 per cent of low-income seniors being women
- Beware of debt holes from credit card debt, retail therapy, health issues, job loss, caretaking, time off, poor decisions, or bad relationships

- Glass ceilings are part of this picture, as women earn far less because of lack of advancement. It also costs women more that men to support themselves at the same level of comfort because of the so-called gender tax with higher prices for many items and services like haircuts, for example
- Life expectancy is higher for women and on less money to boot
- Caregiving roles often fall to women who can go part time or take time off to care for others, which reduces their pensions and savings
- Women are more likely to need long-term care and assisted living. They definitely experience longevity risk, as well as market and inflation risk
- Women's standard of living drops with a divorce or separation and widowhood. Divorcees have lower replacement income than widows do
- The median age of becoming a widow in Canada is 56, and a single woman needs 66 per cent of a couple's income to maintain the same lifestyle
- Common-law marriages require careful estate planning as the same protections or legal rights are not in place
- Spousal Old Age Security ends with a husband's death, and other pensions may be greatly reduced or disappear, as well
- Finding a trusted advisor is also a problem for many. Rob Carrick of the *Globe and Mail*, in an article, "Is Anybody Listening?", wrote about problems of communication between males who dominate the industry and female clients. About 70 per cent of females are dissatisfied with their advisors and do switch after the death of a spouse

So ...

- Women have lower financial literacy scores than men, and those with lower scores tend to do less planning. Most do not know what they will need or have a goal for retirement income
- Find a women's investment club or group. Educate yourself about your financial and investment options
- You may not be able to prevent costly long-term health conditions, but you can prepare
- Beware of caregiving that reduces earnings and savings, putting you in a vulnerable position

- The Baby Boom women are the first generation of career women to have any studies done about their experiences of retirement; their invisibility has continued until now
- Take responsibility for your financial future, get your legal and financial ducks in a row, find trusted advisors to work with, and keep your retirement in mind when making serious decisions
- Start now and tackle debt, monitor accounts, organize paperwork, work out a savings and investment strategy, check sites like getsmarteraboutmoney and retirehappy.ca as you tend your financial garden
- Think of yourself as a wealth builder, and keep your eye on the money ball
- On the bright side, despite their finances, women tend to get happier as they age. They have stronger social networks, too. However, a head-in-the-sand approach does not work. Financial resources and knowledge do provide peace of mind and confidence

Spousal Old Age Security benefits end with a partner's death. Some widows/widowers receive a survivor benefit from CPP/QPP unless they are receiving the maximum payment based on their own work.

You need to understand survivor benefits of CPP/QPP, OAS, and your partner's pension. When a spouse dies, income is reduced while expenses often remain the same.

The basics:

- The earlier you invest your money, the more time it has to grow. Small regular contributions add up
- Maximize annual RRSP contributions and use the tax savings to reduce debt or invest further
- Know your company pension plan. When looking for a new job, be sure to research the pension plan
- Avoid debt. Pay off highest-interest debt first. Know your credit rating
- Learn about investing and risk. The more you educate yourself, the more confident you'll be in dealing with advisors
- Get good, independent professional advice. Studies show a better financial picture for those who work with financial planners

GUERRILLA FRUGALITY

- Budget – track your expenses and match them with your net income
- Reduce expenses – housing and vehicles are the biggest ticket items
- Get out of debt as quickly as possible
- Keep a spending diary
- Walk/bike/use public transit, try car sharing or car rental
- Bundle to save on TV, cable, telephone
- Check insurance costs
- Cut energy costs – insulate pipes, wear a sweater, use power bars and turn them off when not needed, use timers and weather stripping, plant trees, get rid of old appliances, use a programmable thermostat, change filters, clean vents, replace old light bulbs
- Rent out a room or suite in your house, or rent rather than own
- Downsize, have a garage sale, put ads on Kijiji
- Cook from scratch
- Plan menus and shop accordingly
- Shop with a list
- Use coupons and shop for sales
- Use seasonal produce, the closer to the source the better, and dry, can, or preserve
- Freeze produce or dishes for later
- Price-compare – particularly for travel
- Take that seniors discount
- Sort out need from wants
- Make and meet savings goals
- Join the DIY movement
- Fix, trade, find a used replacement
- Join and use the library
- Pay off credit cards monthly

RETIRING FROM THE FARM

Farm operations like many businesses have implications for succession and transition planning along with retirement planning. Figuring out who will take over from either family or non-family members can be a challenge and a straight sale can be complicated, as well.

Getting professional valuations, finding out tax implications, dealing with the farm corporation if there is one, and sorting out wills, powers of attorney, estate planning, and legacy that is fair to farm and non-farm adult children can be daunting. All succession plans are different and require serious consideration to deal with capital gains, taxes, various assets that may include quotas, a corporation, a principal residence, as well as the OAS clawback, insurance, timing, and family circumstances and wishes.

That is why many farmers put off dealing with these issues often until a crisis forces some decisions be made. This can come in the form of a health crisis, a death, a request or even a threat from a family member or members, or a financial challenge. With the average age of farmers at 55 years, the time for planning is now or yesterday! Denial is costly in terms of both dollars and mental anguish.

Sadly, too many farm businesses run into trouble when the principal owner dies without the proper paperwork in place to make a smooth transition. This jeopardizes the farm business and can lead to bitter family disputes. If the issue is a health-related one, especially without proper insurance or back-up help, the transition can be rushed and flawed and be a stressful burden on others. Too many families become splintered as a result of poor planning or no forethought at all.

Start by thinking about what retirement is going to look like. It is not being put out to pasture. Active retirement is just that...active. Consider where you may be living, as a severance may be required. Think about your involvement with the farm as part time or not at all. Get to your banker, insurance broker, lawyer, tax preparer, and accountant and start to put a succession plan together. Have a transition period to allow getting full value from farm assets, carry out the succession plan, train the next generation, or ease out at your own pace.

Communicate your thoughts with your spouse and children and get their feedback. Include the sons-in-law and daughters-in-law, as well. In one case, a farmer sold his farm and announced the news to his son-in-law, who had been farming with him for eight years, on his way back from the lawyer's office. Not much contact with grandchildren since!

Farmers often have much of their identities wrapped up in what they do, what they own, the family history of farming, and their communities. Lots of options exist for doing related activities from mentoring with groups like Farm Management Canada's Step-up Program, 4-H or Junior Farmers, to volunteering at plowing matches and service clubs, or starting a related business. Reflect on what you want to do with your time, energy, experience, and interests and fill up your soul and not just your day.

One banker stated that many farmers consider retirement somewhere on the scale from castration to euthanasia. That is just plain wrong! The biggest mistakes farmers make, besides this kind of attitude, are not having an up-to-date will, lacking succession or transition plans, failing to hold family discussions, treating family members unfairly, or bending over backwards for their children and not looking after themselves. Planning ahead can help avoid these problems.

PHILANTHROPY AND LEGACY

Many Canadians donate their time, energy, and money to groups that reflect their values and interests. Those values may be community, innovation, justice, spirituality, freedom, or many more. Those interests may be civil rights, arts and culture, hospitals, disaster relief, domestic violence, human rights, the environment, or so many others. The variety of opportunities to make a positive difference is wide-ranging.

Canadians want their resources used efficiently and effectively whether it is an end-of-life-bequest or a present offering. Charity Intelligence is a site that rates and reviews Canadian charities. Other watchdogs provide information to potential donors. Tax credits serve to encourage giving, as well.

Donations tend to increase with age and are more likely from those who do volunteer work. Those in the three western provinces of Canada are the most generous as are the best educated across the country. Religious institutions get the most money, with healthcare facilities next. According to the CRA, in 2012 Canadians gave $8.3 billion. One interesting trend is the increase in female donors, who now outnumber male donors.

The percentage of volunteer hours was 53 per cent by women and 47 per cent by men for the 2.1 billion volunteer hours as of 2010, according to Statistics Canada. These are on the increase as Boomers are looking for meaningful and purposeful activities.

One retired executive explained why he would never go to another meeting. He bags groceries at a food bank; another woman was looking for an arts organization where she could offer her skills on the board. Figure out what you want to support with time or money or both. Do your homework and get involved.

This may be part of your estate planning. Check getsmarteraboutmoney.ca for provincial differences and get expert advice.

We make a living by what we get but we make a life by what we give.

~WINSTON CHURCHILL

FINANCIAL ✓ CHECKLIST

- ❑ Track spending for a year
- ❑ Assess present financial situation
- ❑ Check into your pension in terms of timing and projected amount
- ❑ Get estimates for CPP/QPP for various ages of retirement
- ❑ Research benefits options
- ❑ Meet with banker/financial planner about your present financial situation
- ❑ Develop a financial plan
- ❑ Understand the effects of inflation
- ❑ Look into insurance needs and options
- ❑ Update your will
- ❑ Assign powers of attorney for property and for personal care
- ❑ Complete your living will
- ❑ Look into your housing and transportation options
- ❑ Do your estate planning with a qualified, experienced legal advisor
- ❑ Research your credit rating
- ❑ Investigate survivor benefits
- ❑ Assess your timing options for retirement
- ❑ Play sick and dead and follow what would happen
- ❑ Investigate options for renovations or relocation
- ❑ Look into options for part-time employment
- ❑ Consider starting a business
- ❑ Investigate phased retirement as an option
- ❑ Consider timing for drawing down an RRSP
- ❑ Use benefits now for dental work, glasses, orthotics
- ❑ Fix up your house before retirement

- ❑ Buy your next car before retiring
- ❑ Research OAS, tax credits, income splitting, tax deferral
- ❑ Look into the implications of snowbirding for taxes, insurance needs, and housesitting

Women in North America pay anywhere from 30 to 50 per cent more for goods and services like haircuts, alterations, cars, cosmetics, contracting services and dry-cleaning.

~JOANNE THOMAS YACCATO, *BALANCING ACT*

Section Three

Health and Wellness

HEALTH TIPS AND FACTS

Health is the biggest reason people choose to retire. A health threat and the negative effects of stress can lead to a re-evaluation of what is important and precipitate a choice to retire. The health of someone close – a spouse, a parent – can also be the deciding factor.

In 1900, the average life span was 47.3 years. The age for retirement went from 70 to 65 when the average man lived to 63 and average woman to 66. Now retirement can last as long as work life or longer.

People who exercise:

- Feel better
- Have more energy
- Require less sleep
- Have improved muscular strength and flexibility
- Maintain a healthy weight
- Decrease their anxiety and depression
- Enhance their self-esteem
- Improve their digestion
- Enhance their body mechanics
- Improve their blood circulation and oxygenation
- Breathe more efficiently
- Reduce their heart rate
- Boost mental acuity and mood
- Elevate neurotransmitters like serotonin and dopamine

Consider some sobering facts about the health of seniors:

- The three top causes of death are heart disease, cancer, and stroke

- If you followed 100 people born in the 1940s and 50s, the mortality would average:
  By age 16 – one lost
  From age 63 and on – you begin to lose one per year
  By age 75 – 67 left
  By age 100 – three left
- About 43 per cent of Canadians 65-plus take five or more prescriptions
- Health-care costs may rise to pay for in-home assistance, equipment for reduced mobility, home renovation, or a move to an assisted living residence
- Expect to become more sensitive to heat and cold, and to medicines, alcohol, and tobacco
- Expect to need less food, less sleep, and more rest
- Work to maintain muscle mass and calcium in bones and teeth
- Learn to cope with relocation, illness, and death of loved ones
- Set up a notebook for jotting down ideas, names, numbers, questions
- Keep in mind that 70 per cent of total lifetime health-care costs occur in the last ten years of life
- Factor in that health spending has risen since 2008 by more than 5 per cent, or about $9.5 billion, before inflation

HEALTH IS THE WILD CARD

- A health condition can result in loss of employment income, increased costs for professionals like a physiotherapist or massage therapist, and extra expenses for prescription drugs, special equipment purchase or rental, and in-home care. These can add to the financial burden on top of the emotional stress
- Health issues like cognitive decline, deterioration of vision or hearing, reduced muscle control or the introduction of walkers or wheelchairs may mean home redesign and renovation or relocation
- The family can take on additional expenses or take time from work for caretaking and extra household duties. This can mean going into debt or depleting savings.

A crisis happening after retirement can be challenging with a fixed income with little room for such extras

- Too many have no disability or critical care insurance or just-in-case savings for a health issue. Heart disease and cancer are the most common culprits, and dementia, especially early onset, can poke big holes in a retirement plan, as well as place an enormous burden on caregivers
- Living longer does not mean living disease or pain free. The quality of life deteriorates as health does. According to Statistics Canada, men experience 9.4 years on average of poor quality of life while for females it is 11.8 years
- Long life is now deemed a longevity risk by financial planners as outliving savings becomes an issue and a fear
- A health concern may mean increased needs for care, medications, possible relocation, and medical aids. At the same time, doctors are now putting new knees and hips into 95 year olds so they can continue their active lives
- The demographic bulge that is the Baby Boomers means dramatic pressure on health-care services and personnel. As doctors and nurses retire, experience and knowledge go with them. Shortages of family doctors and gerontologists mean big gaps in medical care. People in northern and rural areas are most likely to be under serviced

Both depression and alcoholism are key health concerns for retirees. One-third of seniors who drink abusively did not start doing so until their retirement.

Age-related restrictions to life activities affect one in five seniors aged 65 to 74, one in three aged 75 to 85, and one in two over 85 years old.

> Those who do not find time for exercise will have to find time for illness.
>
> ~OLD PROVERB

HEALTHY AGING

Highly functional aging adults have in common a positive attitude, engagement in hobbies or activities, and good health.

Be attentive to your mood and attitude. Depression, sadness, and low mood are not a natural part of aging.

Steps you could take to reduce your health risks:

- Don't smoke; smoking is a major cause of cardiovascular disease and bone loss
- Eat a balanced, heart-healthy diet
- Take a daily multivitamin, 1200–1500 mg of calcium, and 800 IU of vitamin D to bolster your bones
- Maintain a healthy weight – being too thin increases the risk of osteoporosis, and being overweight is a risk factor for heart disease, stroke, diabetes, and arthritis
- Have regular checkups to monitor your blood pressure, cholesterol, and glucose levels
- Women over 65 are now advised to take low-dose (81 mg) aspirin every day (or 100 mg every other day) to prevent heart attack and stroke
- Consider getting a yearly flu shot and a pneumococcal vaccine
- Practise moderation in your intake of alcohol, sugar, processed foods, and fat
- Eliminate saturated fats and trans fats, refined sugar, and processed carbs
- Stay positive and engaged

> Singing seems to be both mentally and physically healthy; research suggests that it can increase immune function. It seems to produce endorphins and the feel-good hormone dopamine.
>
> ~DR. MICHAEL ROIZEN AND DR. MEHMET OZ

HEALTH DOWNSIDES OF RETIREMENT

- The greatest negative health effects are generated by involuntary or forced retirement. Many experience financial and emotional stress, with feelings of anger, rejection, loss of self-worth, and grief. They may need counselling and/or connecting to others who have been through it before to make the transition from "the end of the world" to "new beginnings and/or a fresh start"
- A new condition has emerged recently, or at least it has been given a name: "retired husband syndrome" – a syndrome that is causing wives to suffer from stress-related conditions
- Depression and substance abuse are often tied to retirement
- Health is the predominant reason given in the decision to retire. Most choose disability payments to bridge from the decision point to the actual retirement

FOR BETTER HEALTH, FIND YOUR PEOPLE

- Social isolation can be really bad for you. Insomnia, higher blood pressure, and depression, for a start. Social integration, contacts, and networks are vital to personal welfare
- Ellen Langer, a psychology professor at Harvard, put it this way: "If you have a mind-set that everything gets worse as you age and nothing's as good as it was before, then anything that reminds you that you're a senior is going to be negative. But now there's a belief that 80 is the new 60, and so if you get people together who are feeling vital, I think retirement communities can be great places." (*Boston Globe*, March 2016)
- The Sheridan Centre for Elder Research explained it this way: "All research now is that social engagement is key to maintaining physical as well as intellectual acuity as you age"
- We have been given this gift of time. Let's use it in an engaged, meaningful, fun, challenging, and rewarding way. Try meeting some new folks and get involved with whatever fits your values and interests

PROBUS CLUBS are one place to connect with other retired folks. Across Canada, 238 active clubs have thousands of members attending monthly meetings and forming interest groups like canoeing, hiking, theatre, book groups, and much more.

MEETUPS is across Canada and has a large and diverse membership who arrange meetings based on mutual interests. Check out meetup.com in your area and see what is available or start one of your own.

SENIORS CENTRES are places where you can find peers, stay active, get flu shots, join a band, come for lunch, attend lectures, go on trips, watch films, take courses, or play games. Most Boomers do not like the S word but go there anyway. You may be pleasantly surprised.

CANADIAN ASSOCIATION OF RETIRED PERSONS (carp.ca) has about 300,000 members across the country. Join a chapter, get benefits, and take part in advocacy for seniors. CARP also has a media presence with *Zoomer* magazine, radio, and television.

Social networks are essential to health; keep up with friends and make new ones. "Exercise your mind and stay active as much as you can," says Dr. Lee, a director of the geriatrics consult service at New York-Presbyterian Hospital and assistant professor of medicine at the Weill Cornell Medical College of Cornell University. An article in the college's *Women's Health Advisor* newsletter advises: "Keep up with whatever you like to do, whether it's gardening, reading, dancing, going to the gym, doing crossword puzzles, taking classes, volunteering, or still going to work. Don't say, 'I'm old. I can't do it.' A can-do attitude, otherwise known as optimism, is an essential ingredient of successful aging."

TOP HEALTH ISSUES AFFECTING WOMEN

Women live longer than men. But don't get too excited about this statistic. According to Health Canada, only 2.5 of those years will be disability free. Women may have longer lives, but they aren't necessarily healthier ones.

> The idea is to die young as late as possible.
>
> ~Ashley Montague

CARDIOVASCULAR DISEASE

Every seven minutes someone in Canada has a heart attack or stroke, but even more worrisome is the fact that women are more likely to die from a heart attack than men. Cardiovascular disease, including stroke and disease of the blood vessels, is responsible for one-third of all deaths of Canadian women, according to the most recent statistics. Women also seem to be at a greater risk of cardiovascular disease after menopause when they lose the protective effects of estrogen, so preventative measures need to start earlier than previously thought. Up to 80 per cent of premature heart disease and strokes are preventable with healthy behaviours.

BREAST AND LUNG CANCER

Cancer affects more people in Canada than any other disease. According to the latest statistics from the Canadian Cancer Society, 42 per cent of Canadian women will develop cancer during their lifetime.

Breast cancer gets a lot of the attention, and for good reason: it's the most common type of cancer in women. Breast cancer accounts for 26 per cent of all new cancer cases in women. But there is good news: the Canadian Cancer Society notes that both incidence and death rates are on the decline. In other words, fewer women are developing the disease than in past decades, and more women are surviving.

Unfortunately, the same can't be said for the deadliest cancer killer: lung cancer. Over the years, rates of this cancer in women have risen to the point of almost equalling men's. Only half as many women will be diagnosed with lung cancer as with breast cancer, but nearly twice as many will die from it. Worse yet, the majority of these cases are preventable because they are caused by smoking.

Colorectal cancer is the third after breast and lung cancer in women. Skin cancer is also an increasing risk. We can do a lot of things to minimize our risk, like eating plenty of fruits and vegetables, exercising, not smoking, and avoiding exposure to sun, radiation, and chemicals. Regular screenings are also essential to detect cancers in their earliest, and most curable, stages. Self-examination needs to be part of a regular routine. Know your family history.

TYPE 2 DIABETES

When you combine the aging population, growing obesity rates, and increasingly sedentary lifestyles, this illness may be a very expensive condition.

However, the personal costs are much higher. Adults with diabetes are twice as likely to die prematurely – by as much as five to 15 years, depending on the type. Diabetes also goes hand-in-hand with other chronic diseases: 80 per cent of people with diabetes will die of heart disease or stroke, and others are more likely to get cancer. Furthermore, diabetes can cause complications like blindness, amputation, and kidney disease, another top cause of death for men and women alike. The rise in obesity rates in women, combined with their already increased risk of chronic diseases, makes diabetes a serious concern in protecting their future health.

People should be on the lookout for the early signs of diabetes. Damage to the body often starts during the "pre-diabetes" phase, but it's not too late to avoid type 2 diabetes at that stage. Visit your doctor if you are experiencing the warning signs of unusual thirst, unexplained weight change, frequent urination, cuts or bruises that are slow to heal, blurred vision, and tingling or numbness in the hands and feet.

MUSCULOSKELETAL DISEASES

These diseases aren't a top cause of death, but they certainly are a top health concern for women. Diseases affecting the bones, joints, and muscles are more common for females. Women are twice as likely as men to develop arthritis in general and rheumatoid arthritis in particular. Currently, 19 per cent of women live with arthritis versus 11 per cent of men. By 2026, an estimated one in four women will be affected. By age 75, over 50 per cent of women have arthritis. Women also have a greater risk of certain types of bone and joint diseases. They're four times as likely to develop fibromyalgia, and they account for 90 per cent of the people who develop lupus, a potentially fatal autoimmune disease. Women are also twice as likely to suffer from osteoporosis, partly due to the loss of bone following menopause. Currently, one in four women over the age of 50 lives with the disease.

MENTAL HEALTH

Experts note that while mental illness affects people of all ages, walks of life, gender, and race, women experience it differently. For instance:

- Women are more likely to suffer from anxiety disorders and depression
- Women are more likely to have been victims of incest, sexual abuse, battery, and violence. They're also more likely to develop an eating disorder
- Women find it harder to maintain good a work-life balance and are more affected by stress at work and home

- While more men commit suicide, women make more attempts

Not only do some women face the prejudice of being "weak" or "emotional," they also have to face the consequences of being treated like a man. Experts warn that doctors need to factor in women's hormonal changes, whether they're due to menstruation, pregnancy, or menopause, rather than dismissing women because of them.

While the causes of mental illness are complex, there are some simple things people can do for better mental health. These include reducing stress, maintaining a good work-life balance, and seeking support when needed, especially during life-altering events like the death of a loved one or divorce. And don't overlook the essentials like daydreaming, laughing, and exercising. Check out information from the Canadian Mental Health Association (cmha.ca).

Experts recommend that people should also be aware of the warning signs of mental illness and shouldn't be afraid to seek help. Get past the stigma – after all, one in five Canadians will experience a mental illness at some point during their lives. Women shouldn't be afraid to insist on the treatment they need as individuals.

MENOPAUSE

After menopause, a woman's metabolism slows down permanently. Body fat is stored on the abdomen, which is dangerous. Waist measurement that exceeds 35 inches is a risk. Obesity rates for women 55 to 59 have quadrupled in the last 15 years to about 20 per cent. Depressing and unfair as this may seem, steps to boost metabolism can help.

SUGGESTIONS FOR BOOSTING METABOLISM

- Exercise regularly – aerobic, flexibility, strength, balance
- Eat spicy foods (capsaicin in peppers and curry boost metabolism), as well as almonds and dairy products like yogurt
- Eat lean protein
- Reduce portions
- Eat breakfast
- Stay hydrated, but avoid plastic containers
- Eat lighter meals later in the day because the metabolic rate is like the shape of an ice cream cone – big at the top in the morning and tapering off through the day
- Get your seven to eight hours of sleep

- Drink seven to eight glasses of water daily
- Reduce stress – cortisol, a stress-related hormone, slows metabolism
- Know your BMI core – Body Mass Index calculators are available online
- Know your Waist to Hip Ratio (WHR)
- Check out Hormone Replacement Therapy (womenshealthmatters.com) – to HRT or not to HRT

THE "P" WORD

Many of you cross your legs to sneeze and know the location of every bathroom on your travel routes. Estrogen loss affects muscle quality. Kegel exercises and Pilates can help restore muscle control. Medication and surgery may also help; you may wish to consult your doctor concerning tipped bladder or bladder control.

WOMEN AND LONG-TERM HEALTH

Women, on average, live longer than men. However, a long retirement may be a mixed blessing if bad health affects the quality of that retirement.

Women are more likely than men to develop costly long-term health problems. These may require personal care, a different living situation or modifications to the present one, and higher prescription or medical equipment costs. It is also possible that long-term care insurance may be denied because of a pre-existing condition, leaving women vulnerable on many levels. Maintenance programs and strong social support networks are crucial during these vulnerable periods.

TOP HEALTH ISSUES AFFECTING MEN

CANCER

Some 45 per cent of Canadian men will develop cancer during their lifetimes – a rate that's 5 per cent higher than in women.

The most common type of cancer in men, prostate cancer, occurs at a higher rate than breast cancer does in women. One in seven men will have it, and one in 27 will die from it. Skin cancer is also a risk. And while lung cancer rates in men have been declining, the disease still kills more men than women. Despite the fact that lung cancer occurs half as often as prostate cancer, it will kill twice as many men. The obvious ways to lower the risk: Don't smoke, quit smoking, avoid second-hand smoke.

Colorectal cancer, despite being the third most common cancer in both males and females, has a higher incidence and death rate in men.

What can be done to minimize the risks? Healthy lifestyle choices like eating a balanced diet, exercising, not smoking, and maintaining a healthy weight are essential, as is avoiding unnecessary exposure to radiation and chemicals. Regular screenings like a PSA or DRE test for prostate cancer are also helpful to detect cancers in their earliest, and most curable, stages. Regular checkups and doctor visits help with early detection. Denial is not an alternative to proper care; too many men wait until their symptoms are quite uncomfortable.

HEART DISEASE AND STROKE

Statistics show that eight in ten people have at least one risk factor for cardiovascular disease, but some of these risk factors show up more often in men. For example, men are more likely to be smokers and to be overweight or obese. Also, men in certain age groups are more at risk than women who have some protective benefits from estrogen before menopause.

In addition, most victims of cardiac arrest – which is almost always fatal when it happens outside of a hospital – are men in their late 60s or early 70s.

The good news is that cardiovascular disease is on the decline; however, both men and women can do more to prevent it. Following all of the usual advice – a healthy diet, maintaining a normal weight, regular physical activity, stress management, not smoking, and cutting back on the salt – can reduce the risk. The risk does rise with age, however.

TYPE 2 DIABETES

Men are more likely to develop diabetes than women. According to Statistics Canada, more men have diabetes than women in most age groups, with the exception of those 75 and over. Thanks to rising obesity rates and increasingly sedentary lifestyles, this disease is one of the fastest growing in Canada.

While the disease can be managed, it can still rob people of five to 15 years of their lifespan. People with diabetes are more likely to develop other chronic illnesses, and an estimated 80 per cent will die of heart disease or stroke. Diabetes can also lead to other complications resulting in blindness, amputation, and kidney disease.

What's troublesome about these numbers is that about 90 per cent of all diabetes cases are type 2 diabetes. In other words, most of the cases could be prevented with good lifestyle choices with regard to diet, weight, and exercise. According to research, people over 50 can reduce their risk by 58 per cent simply by exercising moderately for 30 minutes per day and losing 5 to 7 per cent of their body weight. People over 60 who do the same thing can cut their risk by as much as 71 per cent.

Knowing the early warning signs is also essential. Damage to the body can start to occur during the pre-diabetes stage, but it's not too late to stop type 2 diabetes from developing. As mentioned earlier, be on the lookout for symptoms like unexplained weight changes, frequent urination, unusual thirst, wounds that are slow to heal, blurred vision, and tingling or numbness in the hands and feet. When in doubt, seek help. As with other chronic conditions, the earlier the diagnosis and treatment, the better.

SUICIDE

More women suffer from anxiety and depression than men, but the latest numbers from Statistics Canada show a grim trend when it comes to men's mental health. Suicide is the seventh-leading cause of death for men – placing it ahead of Alzheimer's disease, kidney disease, and the flu. Suicide is a silent epidemic.

In many countries like Canada, the U.S., and Australia, men are three to four times more likely to commit suicide than women.

And it's not a matter of student-aged angst. Suicide rates among men in the 40 to 60 and over 80 age groups are higher than in teens and early 20s. Rates are three times higher among Canada's aboriginal peoples compared with the general population.

The reasons behind suicide are complex, and there's some controversy as to why more men than women kill themselves. For instance, some experts argue that men are less likely to seek help than women, or they may understate their problems in order to not seem vulnerable.

However, the important thing is that suicide can be prevented if the symptoms and risks can be identified in time. Some of the warning signs include depression, remarks related to dying, giving away possessions, making preparations for death, or a sudden switch in attitude from being hopeless to being cheerful. (Once the person has made the decision to commit suicide, he or she tends to show a positive attitude. People are relieved that the person is "getting better" and then are shocked by the act of suicide.)

ERECTILE DYSFUNCTION

It's not a cause of death, and it can be "fixed" with one of those medications you see in the media – so what's it doing on this list? Women may joke that men put too much stock in their anatomy, but the fact is, erectile dysfunction, or impotence, is often a warning sign of more serious health problems. As many as one-third of men face ED, and it's most common after the age of 65. Diabetes and some medications can be causes.

While the symptoms can affect a man's sex life – not to mention his well-being and self-image – it's the underlying cause that's a concern. A pattern of not being able to get or keep an erection can be caused by diseases and conditions that affect the nerves, brain, and blood vessels. For example, impotence can be a symptom of diabetes or pre-diabetes. ED is often caused by atherosclerosis (hardening of the arteries, which can lead to heart disease), high blood pressure, and liver or kidney failure. Alcohol abuse and smoking can also cause ED, as can high levels of stress. Take a look at the quality of relationship with the intimate partner, as well.

The bottom line: Men who are experiencing erectile dysfunction should see their doctor to make sure the causes of ED are treated, not just the symptoms. Men who would like to avoid the problem altogether should maintain a healthy weight, stop smoking, and keep their cholesterol and blood pressure at healthy levels. Men with diabetes will need to keep their condition under control, too.

TAKE CARE

It's more than just aches and pains. The diseases described above eat away at people's independence and quality of life, and they're extremely costly to society thanks to long-term disability costs and lost productivity. These diseases take an emotional toll, as well, and symptoms may include fatigue and depression.

While many of these diseases aren't preventable, people can do a lot to delay their onset or deal with the symptoms. Getting plenty of calcium is important, especially for children and young adults, to help prevent osteoporosis. Plenty of exercise, maintaining a healthy weight, and eating a balanced diet can help put a hold on some types of arthritis like osteoarthritis and can help manage symptoms when they do occur. Losing even as little as ten pounds can significantly reduce stress on the body. Physical fitness means feeling better, looking better, and sleeping better.

THE AGING PROCESS

The effects of aging vary greatly among individuals. Although differences are reported between men and women, many of the changes will normally occur in most people. Inherited qualities play a major role, although lifestyle factors such as smoking, exercise, and nutrition can all affect the aging process.

- **Heart:** Grows slightly larger. For men, the heart's ability to pump oxygen during exercise declines by 5 per cent to 10 per cent for each decade of adult life. For women, it declines by 7.6 per cent. Women, who tend to develop coronary heart disease and hypertension later than men, may experience more angina attacks
- **Blood pressure:** Size of blood vessels narrows. Systolic blood pressure – the top number – increases by about 15 per cent between the ages of 35 and 70. What is considered normal is a systolic pressure, when the heart muscle is contracted, of 120 over a diastolic pressure, when the heart muscle is relaxed, of 80
- **Lungs:** Maximum breathing capacity can decline by 40 per cent between ages of 20 and 70
- **Sight:** Inability to focus close up can start in the 40s. Ability to see the fine details decreases in the 70s
- **Taste:** The number of taste buds can decline, causing an inability to appreciate subtle distinctions in flavours
- **Smell:** Declines slowly after age 45 and more rapidly after 65, making it difficult to detect delicate fragrances
- **Hearing:** Ability to hear higher frequencies declines. Hearing loss occurs less rapidly in women than in men
- **Skin:** Loses its elasticity because of declines in collagen, a connective tissue. Exposure to environmental factors such as sunlight and wind can cause dryness

If exercise could be packed into a pill, it would be the single most widely prescribed and beneficial medicine in the world.

~ROBERT BUTLER, M.D.

- **Hair:** As people age, the body produces less colour pigment, triggering the graying process. This becomes more noticeable after age 30
- **Nerves:** The production of neurotransmitters – chemical messengers that carry impulses to and from the brain – slows down. A loss of peripheral nerves can blunt the sense of touch, pain, and sensitivity to heat and cold. Changes in nerves in the inner ear can cause dizziness, making it difficult to maintain balance
- **Memory:** Declines slightly. Older women are significantly better at recalling words, and older men are much better at recalling numbers
- **Personality:** No changes reported unless a disease, such as Alzheimer's, which affects memory and mood, is present
- **Male reproductive system:** The male hormone testosterone steadily diminishes Changes in hormone balance may cause an enlargement of prostate gland, which produces the fluid in semen
- **Female reproductive system:** The ovarian sex hormones, estrogen and progesterone, decline after age 50. This can accelerate bone loss in women, which can cause osteoporosis and an increased risk of fractures. Hot flashes may also result
- **Sexual function:** In men, sexual activity tends to decline with age. Men who had more frequent sex as young adults continue that pattern after age 40. For women, aging has little effect on sexual pleasure, although desire and frequency of orgasm may decrease with age
- **Kidneys and bladder:** Gradual reduction in blood flow to the kidneys impairs their ability to extract wastes from the blood. Bladder capacity also declines. In women, loss of muscle strength can cause urinary incontinence
- **Immune system:** The thymus, a gland that regulates T cells, which help fight off disease, gradually shrinks. As the gland fades away, the number of T cells decline. The ability to release antibodies to fight off infections also decreases
- **Body fat:** Women have 50 per cent more body fat than men and store it in the hips-buttocks-thigh areas. Men store fat in the abdominal area. With age, the body does not normally lose fat but will redistribute it from just under the skin to deeper parts of the body
- **Teeth and gums:** Presence of gingivitis – inflammation of the gums – and periodontal disease – inflammation of the tissues that support the teeth – increases with age

- **Muscles:** Muscle mass declines between 20 per cent, and 40 per cent with a lack of exercise
- **Bones:** Men and women begin to lose bone mass after 40. One in eight men over 60 have osteoporosis. One of every four women over age 60 and half over age 70 have osteoporosis severe enough to cause pain, loss of weight, and spinal deformity. One in every ten will break a hip by age 80. Some 30 per cent will die of complications, and half of those who could walk before they broke their hip will be permanently crippled
- **Height:** Men and women tend to shrink with age, due to alterations in bone structure and muscle tissue. The change is more severe in women muscle tone with age. Regular contractions that propel food through the system become less frequent, causing the stomach to take longer to process it. The gallbladder also slows down, releasing bile into the small intestine and increasing the likelihood of gallstones. The liver shrinks

CARPE DIEM!

According to Frederick Vettese's book *The Essential Retirement Guide*, released in 2016, 50 year olds in Canada have a 50-50 chance of getting to age 70 without dying or suffering a critical illness like cancer, heart disease, or many other conditions. This is for males because the research for females is just not there.

The top six of these are: cancer, heart disease, dementia, stroke, Parkinson's disease, and kidney failure. Quality of life can certainly be diminished by other serious health problems like arthritis, diabetes, osteoporosis, results of accidents, ear or eye issues, mental illness, and other maladies the flesh is heir to in the course of a long life.

We may be living longer but not necessarily in good health for the duration. The active part of retirement can come to a sudden halt before you have ticked off much on the bucket list. No one wants regrets on the deathbed. Go for your best possible retirement with gusto while you can.

RISK FACTORS AND HEALTH

1. Smoking.
2. High blood pressure and cholesterol.
3. Lack of physical activity.
4. High body mass index (BMI).
5. High glucose.
6. Exposure to low-quality air, water, pollution, toxins, too much sun.
7. Over-medication by legal and/or illegal drugs.
8. Excessive intake of alcohol.
9. Poor nutrition including high trans fats, sodium, and processed foods and low intake of fruit, vegetables, nuts, seeds, and other high-nutrition value sources.
10. Poor sleep patterns, sleep debt.

COUNTERING HEALTH RISK FACTORS

1. Quit smoking.
2. Do monitoring, get checkups.
3. Have a fitness regime and be active for 30 minutes a day minimum.
4. Reduce stress.
5. Eat a modified Mediterranean-style diet.
6. Include organic produce, whole grains, pulses, fish, fibre, monounsaturated fats.
7. Reduce or eliminate artificial sweeteners, white carbohydrates, sugars, and trans fats, and read labels on food packaging.
8. Have social supports, friends and family, interest groups.
9. Get seven to eight hours of sleep a day.
10. Reduce body fat if that is a factor.
11. Know your genetic risk factors as well as the lifestyle ones.

12. Build a health-care team.

13. Have a self-care routine and plan.

14. Challenge your brain daily.

15. Healthy sexual activity has positive effects at many levels.

A good sense of humour and opportunities to laugh can boost the immune system, lower blood sugar levels, and help manage pain. Learn some jokes or funny stories, watch funny movies, be more playful, listen to comedy shows, and learn to laugh at yourself.

Statistically, men have chronic conditions by age 67 and women by age 70. One in three will have a disability, and by age 75 that increases to one in two. Perceptual problems like hearing and vision loss as well as memory loss may restrict options.

Age-related macular degeneration (AMD) is the main cause of vision loss for those over 50; by age 75, one in three will have AMD to some extent. Multivitamins with lutein support eye health.

Energy levels decline with time, as well. Less sleep but more rest is the reality for many.

Even limited training in mindfulness and meditation improves cognitive skills, allowing a person to switch off the stress response, shift focus away from internal chatter, and refocus on the here and now.

A positive attitude and mood reduces the stress hormone cortisol, and, in women, lowers blood levels of proteins associated with inflammation that can contribute to heart disease and cancer.

The rate of HIV has doubled for the 50-plus age group!

TWO "S" WORDS...SEX AND SENIORS

Boomers do not like that seniors word, but we are big fans of the other one! Look at all the busy dating sites for the over-50 crowd. Many are looking for companionship, a life partner, a sexual partner, or some combination. The urges to love and be loved are ageless.

Sex has lots of pluses like improved mood, sleep, circulation, and immune system function. It releases hormones like human growth hormone, testosterone, estrogen, endorphins, and oxytocin. Intimacy is a human need, and sex may be its most powerful expression.

An American study published in the *New England Journal of Medicine* states:

- Of those aged 57 to 64, 73 per cent were sexually active
- Aged 65 to 75, 53 per cent were
- Aged 76 to 85, 26 per cent were
- The average frequency was two to three times per month
- One of seven men used Viagra, Cialis, or a related product
- Women were often not active because of a lack of partner, not a lack of interest

The main barriers as the aging process advances are impotency in men and unavailability of partners for women. Lori Brotto, a registered psychologist and University of British Columbia associate professor of gynecology, warns of the rising rates of STIs like chlamydia, gonorrhea, and syphilis, including in retirement communities and nursing homes! Rates of HIV and other STIs have doubled in a decade for the 50-plus age group. Testing is free and available although not the most romantic start to a relationship.

The e-book *The Later Dater* by Valerie Gibson warns women to carry condoms and not assume exclusivity with their partners. A Public Health nurse I interviewed said, "Somebody needs to let them know about the minefield of consequences. Pregnancy is no longer one, but there are lots more."

Sexual activity has a number of health benefits but make sure to use protection and be careful out there.

Lower hormonal levels including testosterone, health issues, and side effects from some medications can influence libido. The same holds true for problems in the relationship. Sexual intimacy is difficult when a person is self-conscious about a changing body resulting in a poor body image. High stress levels can lead to fatigue, irritability, lethargy, sleep problems, and the physical and mental collapse that is burnout. Sex then takes a backseat. Each of these can reduce confidence, interest, and ability to respond.

THE SCOURGE OF DEMENTIA

- Between 10 and 15 per cent of Canadians live with some form of cognitive impairment. This is due to double by 2031. The risk doubles every five years after 65 and puts enormous strain on families, caregivers, and health-care systems
- Although Alzheimer's disease is the one the majority of dementia sufferers

have, other types do exist. Vascular dementia, dementia with Lewy Bodies, Frontotemporal dementia, and mild cognitive impairment cover the range of types

- In many cases, the person is physically fine, but behaviour changes can be increasingly challenging and, at times, dangerous. Incidents of patient-on-patient violence and patient-on-health-care-worker violence are examples. Family members are also at risk
- The Alzheimer's Society of Canada estimates the medical costs and lost earnings are about $33 million and rising annually
- Between 2 and 10 per cent of all cases of dementia start before age 65, and some people get it in their 40s and 50s. John Mann, the co-founder and vocalist for *Spirit of the West,* is one example. The book by Lisa Genova and movie starring Julianne Moore called *Still Alice* give an excellent window into the effects of this brutal disease
- Risk factors include smoking, high blood pressure and cholesterol, diabetes, obesity, a sedentary lifestyle, depression, head injuries, lack of stimulation, and excessive use of alcohol. Whereas a healthy lifestyle is best for the brain, resistance can be built to a degree by reducing stress, improving nutrition and fitness, challenging the brain, and socializing; however, there are no guarantees for prevention
- Check out the *Brain Bulletin* by Terry Small
- My mother had Lewy Body dementia, and I watched it rob her of sleep, peace of mind, and confidence. She became uncharacteristically apathetic, confused, and anxious. She had hallucinations that disoriented her regularly
- The burden of dementia on families, the health-care and service sectors, care facilities, and taxpayers is growing dramatically and will continue to do so

RECOGNIZING DEMENTIA

The boom is on us as the first of Canada's ten million Baby Boomers turned 65 in 2011. Because the prevalence of Alzheimer's disease and other forms of dementia increases with age, the number of people who suffer its debilitating effects will grow. If you recognize the following warning signs in yourself or a loved one, see a doctor.

- Memory loss that's disruptive to daily life
- Difficulty planning or solving problems

- Difficulty performing familiar tasks
- Being confused about the time or place
- Having trouble understanding visual or spatial relationships
- Having problems with speaking or writing
- Misplacing items or losing belongings in unusual places
- Poor or decreased judgement
- Withdrawal from activities once enjoyed
- Mood or personality changes
- Gait, motor, and balance problems
- Inappropriate behaviour and mood swings

EXERCISE THE GRAY MATTER

One huge problem looming for health care is dementia, a terrifying and debilitating condition. Onset can be delayed through brain maintenance, including:

- Cognitive exercises (research/plan a trip, look into family roots, memorize passages or poetry, play Jeopardy)
- Board games or card games (like Scrabble, bridge, Boggle, chess, euchre)
- Playing music, dancing, or joining a choir
- Taking courses (art, acting, cooking, a new language, a new musical instrument)
- Playing Wii games
- Reducing stress
- Quitting smoking
- Controlling your blood pressure and cholesterol levels
- Exercising (Tai Chi, aerobics, or walking)
- Challenging your brain by reading books, doing research online, or joining Toastmasters, a storytelling group, or a drama club

WORK IT OUT

Dr. Paul Bendheim, a neurologist and author of *The Brain Training Revolution: A Proven Workout for Healthy Brain Aging*, says: "Moderate aerobic activity for 30 minutes three times a week can help you remember better, think better and reduce your risk of Alzheimer's disease, but better blood flow is only part of the answer." To really make the most of your body-brain workout, you can get memory-improving benefits by:

- Vigorous exercise, which boosts mood and increases neurotransmission, blood flow, and oxygenation rates
- Changing up your exercise routine, rotating in a new activity every week
- Tossing a ball or beanbag from hand to hand while you're walking or riding a stationary bike
- Working on your coordination and balance with moves that require a bit of concentration, such as lifting your right toe to touch your left hand
- Exercising outdoors in a natural setting
- Walking or working out with a friend or family member
- Trying some Brain Gym or Train the Brain activities

Exercise increases energy levels and improves sleep, but there is no sure way to prevent dementia.

FOOD FOR THOUGHT

While an overall healthy diet is important for your well-being, specific foods can have brain-boosting benefits. "The key players in neuro-degenerative changes are inflammation and free-radical mediated damage," says Dr. David Perlmutter, a neurologist and co-author of *The Better Brain Book*.

A diet rich in omega-3 fatty acids, specifically DHA, can help protect your neurons, reduce inflammation, and reduce the damage caused by free radicals. "That's why fish is called brain food," he says. "It's rich in DHA, and people who eat the highest levels of fish have the least incidence of Alzheimer's disease."

Antioxidants, including vitamins C and E and beta carotene, can also help neutralize free radicals.

To feed your brain:

- Get 900 to 1,000 milligrams per day of omega-3 fatty acids like DHA by eating limited amounts of cold-water fish such as tuna, salmon, mackerel, and herring, or algae-derived DHA-fortified foods or supplements
- Boost your antioxidant intake, and add broccoli, sweet potatoes, green tea, blueberries, spinach, and turmeric to your diet
- Trade in simple carbohydrates for whole grains such as quinoa, bulgur, couscous, and brown rice
- Nutrition – five a day of foods like walnuts, almonds, colourful berries like blueberries, celery, cocoa, onions, garlic, tomatoes, wild salmon, flax, ginger, green tea, greens, grapes, turmeric, prunes, beans
- Get enough vitamin D

CAREGIVERS

More than 8 million Canadians provide informal care. More than 1 million are over 65 years old. About 1.6 million take time off work to provide care. Over one-quarter of retired women and about 15 per cent of men are caregivers to spouses or other family members. This can be a stressful role, and caregivers need to care for themselves. Here are some tips adapted from a study in the *Journal of Pain and Symptom Management* (June 13, 2007):

1. Take care of yourself, too. Caregiving does not come before your own health, whether physical or mental. Take the time for proper nutrition, exercise, and your own medical appointments. You cannot effectively care for someone else if you need care yourself.
2. Give yourself credit for the work you are doing. You need positive feedback on your efforts. Caretaking can be exhausting, all-encompassing, and unappreciated.
3. Schedule breaks for yourself regularly. Ask for help and relief on a daily basis if possible.
4. Stay in touch with friends and family. This way you won't feel isolated and alone in your role. Ask for some relief time for personal care appointments, exercise, socializing, or personal time.

5. Get support for yourself. This may be from a professional like a counsellor or your doctor or from a peer support group or both. Someone who can relate to you and your experience is invaluable as a sounding board and source of information. You will need reassurance and support from those who understand your situation.

6. Access resources in your community. Consider home-care nursing, Red Cross, Community Care Access Centre, Seniors for Seniors, volunteers, or the local hospice group if this is applicable. Don't try to do everything yourself.

7. Ask for the emotional, practical, and financial support you need. A study by the Canadian Institute for Health Information found that average nursing home care is roughly three times more expensive than care at home.

8. Educate yourself. Knowing everything about your loved one's condition and having a doctor with whom you feel comfortable will help you reduce the unknowns that can cause anxiety and fear. About 35 per cent of working Canadians provide unpaid care. Providing care can be all-encompassing, draining, and overwhelming. The emotional, practical, and financial implications are profound.

FINANCIAL CONSIDERATIONS FOR HEALTH CARE

1. The cost of long-term care facilities can be government subsidized but not the major portion of the cost. Retirement home costs are considerably more, depending on location and services.

2. In case of illness or injury, medical expenses can be expensive for medication, purchase of medical equipment, modification of the home and/or vehicle, and professional or in-home care. Tax benefits may apply but are limited.

3. Also, retirees often lose insurance coverage at retirement. Often they are shocked by the price of replacing group benefit plans. The cost is roughly comparable to insuring a car. Going without coverage can prove to be very expensive because many medical costs are not covered by provincial plans.

4. The cost to employers of extended benefits coverage has resulted in cuts. That means the retiree needs to replace this after doing some research on basic to premium coverage.

5. Taxes may need to be raised as Boomers hit their high medical cost years, peaking in 2031. Gordon Pape, in *Retirement's Harsh New Realities*, says, "We are already

experiencing a 'rationing' of health care. This is having a direct impact on the quality of life of thousands of people."

6. Another problem retirees may experience is addiction, whether to alcohol, prescription drugs, gambling, Internet use, or other substances or behaviours. Help is available.

7. With the high cost of long-term care, many search for options like care by a family member or team of volunteers, paid part-time caregivers, or subsidized long-term care facilities. Rates and eligibility guidelines change depending on which province you are in, length of stay, and type of care and room required. Prices range widely, and competition for these beds can be fierce. The average nursing home care is $126 per day while care at home averages $42 per day.

8. Hospital budgets are under tremendous pressure. Triage choices get made, wait times can stretch on, medical tourism companies book guests, and folks find out how to navigate a complex system to get the care they need or want for themselves or their loved ones.

9. Middle-income Boomers are likely to experience a drop in disposable income and a decline in living standards, and a health crisis can tip this situation into a financial crisis, as well.

10. An Ipsos Reid survey found that 62 per cent of pre-retirees worry about having adequate health care. Very few, however, actually make provisions through insurance or savings.

11. Since Canada's health care is a provincial matter, make sure you have proper travel insurance even within the country. Of course, do not across international borders without it.

12. Take prescribed medications. This may seem odd, but half of Canadians do not take their drugs as prescribed. Ten per cent of hospital visits are the results of drug non-compliance.

13. Ask for generic versions of medications and get a 90-day supply each time to save time and money.

14. Invest in your health with positive, conscious eating choices, regular exercise, and lots of good-quality sleep, and get checkups on a regular basis. Early and accurate diagnoses reduce the duration and cost of health-care issues.

HEALTH-CARE ✓ CHECKLIST

- [ ] I follow an exercise and fitness routine
- [ ] I have educated myself about nutrition and follow a healthy choices diet
- [ ] I know my genetic risk factors
- [ ] I know my lifestyle risk factors
- [ ] I get at least seven hours of quality sleep per night
- [ ] I get regular checkups and blood work done
- [ ] I go to the dentist regularly
- [ ] I go to health-care professionals as needed
- [ ] I monitor my blood pressure, weight, sun exposure, and cholesterol
- [ ] I regularly challenge myself intellectually
- [ ] I have a network of friends and family I can talk to about problems
- [ ] I understand the aging process
- [ ] I have researched health insurance options
- [ ] I have researched post-retirement benefits coverage
- [ ] I have health-care just-in-case savings
- [ ] I understand longevity risk
- [ ] I know my province's health-care benefits
- [ ] I know depression is not a symptom of aging and requires treatment
- [ ] I keep a record of my medications and take them regularly
- [ ] I do not cross provincial or federal borders without adequate insurance coverage

Section Four

Lifestyle

SIX R'S OF RETIREMENT

Revocation

- Consider how to answer your calling and how to use your skills, experience, interests, resources, wisdom, energy, and time
- Look at options with your present employer or business to work in a reduced capacity, change your job description, go part time, work contract to contract or project to project, or become a consultant
- Start your own business or create your own encore career
- Find a different job that may have less stress and more flexibility or may have non-financial perks like club membership in return for hours worked or discounts that you can benefit from

Relocation

- Decisions come into play about where to live and what kind of housing is appropriate
- Aging in place is a popular choice by renovating a home or cottage
- Others choose to stay in their communities but downsize or rent
- Others move to another community in a different part of Canada or to another country
- Some build a granny flat at their own home or that of an offspring
- Some purchase a second property to rent out for another income or for a second home or a combination of both
- Some use their honeymoon period to try out another place to call home. Trying out a new location before buying is a good idea

Regeneration, Reinvention, Redirection, Renewal

- Time to shift gears but not turn off the engine. Find the potential of the Third Quarter of life engaged, inspired, ready to find your purpose, challenge yourself, and keep growing and learning

- Figure out how to age well so the thrill will not be gone
- Figure out what will get you get out of bed in the morning excited about the day
- Rediscover your dreams and make them come true
- Go for the best quality of life you can imagine
- This may require some reflection, self-awareness, experimentation, and research. Take the time to do this for yourself. Those who do not do this risk both their physical and mental health
- Check with Volunteer Canada, Charity Village, or the Canada Volunteer Directory for options to contribute

TIME TO BE INSPIRED

'Tis not too late to seek a newer world . . .
Tho' much is taken, much abides; and tho'
We are not now that strength which in old days
Moved earth and heaven; that which we are, we are . . .
Made weaker by time and fate, but strong in will
To strive, to seek, to find, and not to yield.
(*from "Ulysses," by Alfred Tennyson*)

Build thee more stately mansions, O my soul,
As the swift seasons roll!
Leave thy low-vaulted past!
(*from "The Chambered Nautilus," by Oliver Wendell Holmes*)

It matters not how strait the gate,
How charged with punishments the scroll,
I am the master of my fate;
I am the captain of my soul.
(*William Ernest Henley*)

I did it my way.
(*Paul Anka, sung by Frank Sinatra*)

What Is Success?

To laugh often and love much;
To win the respect of intelligent persons and the affection of children;
To earn the approval of honest critics and endure the betrayal of false friends;
To appreciate beauty;
To find the best in others;
To give of one's self without the slightest thought of return;
To have accomplished a task, whether by a healthy child, a rescued soul, a garden patch or a redeemed social condition;
To have played and laughed with enthusiasm and sung with exaltation;
To know that even one life has breathed easier because you have lived;
This is to have succeeded.
(*Anonymous*)

RECREATION/LEISURE TIPS AND FACTS

Retirement has stages like:

1. Go-go		**1.** Celebration
2. Slow-go	*or*	**2.** Honeymoon
3. No-go		**3.** Coming to terms with a new way of living

The honeymoon period usually lasts six months to two years. You do some of the things you have been putting off or dreaming about: renovating the house, taking a vacation, starting a new fitness routine, visiting family.

It's easy to fall into a rut after the honeymoon retirement stage is over. Keep challenging, exploring, experimenting, and surprising yourself and those who know you. Try something that may seem out of character for you. Don't let the "too old, too shy, too tired, *too whatever*" excuses hold you back.

> The best test of the quality of a civilization is the quality of its leisure.
>
> ~IRWIN EDMAN

You can recalibrate your relationships and forge new routines before as well as after retirement. Begin to seed, to experiment with, to discuss what the new lifestyle will be like. Try on some ideas early. *Bad lifestyle planning can be just as expensive as bad investing.*

The early part of retirement is a period of adjustment, experimentation, and reflection. Major decisions are likely best made after the dust settles a bit. At that point you will have a better vision of your lifestyle, your financial position, and your relationships and social network.

Your new activities happen if they become habits; the sooner these habits are established – pre-retirement, preferably – the easier the transition to full retirement.

You don't need to postpone activities until you retire. Start now. Begin new habits or life choices as early as possible so the transition is easier and more gradual.

We need to satisfy three basic needs:

- Structure
- Purpose
- Sense of community

Prepare for a new future:

- Take courses
- Do some self-assessment
- Research new options
- Gather resources
- Start volunteering
- Daydream, imagine, visualize
- Return to dreams and passions you may have abandoned along the way

Stop living at work and start working at living.

- Consider your choices of how to invest your time, money, and energy
- Research travel destinations and styles
- Renew friendships
- Make some reconnection plans with friends and family

DEMOGRAPHICS

Many of us who are Baby Boomers will be making up new scripts for retirement. Innovation and risk-taking are part of the make-up of this generation. Who knows what retirement will look like as we enter this period in such numbers!

At a demographics conference, a speaker was talking about how bird-watching and gardening were becoming popular activities.

Someone from the back shouted, "Shoot me now!"

The laughter and discussion that followed pointed more to adventure travel and rock concerts.

What will the craft room at the seniors' home look like when we get there?

A friend had a bad fall that resulted in a respite stay. He wanted Wi-Fi in his room, a smart TV, a wider choice on the menu, better exercise and rehab facilities, and a hot tub or sauna available for use. No twelve-channel basic cable and *I Love Lucy* reruns for this generation.

THE FIRST TWO YEARS

During my first two years of my retirement:

I want to pursue ______________________________

I want to try ______________________________

I want to continue ______________________________

I want to research/find out about ______________________________

I want to experiment with ______________________________

I intend to ______________________________

I want to rediscover ______________________________

Travel options:

- House swaps
- Timeshares
- Road Scholar
- Teaching or working abroad
- Vacation exchange clubs
- RVs and campers
- Agency volunteering internationally
- Travel as tour guides

Where do you want to go?

____

____

Benefits of taking courses:

- Increase self-esteem
- Improve mental dexterity
- Structure time
- Meet new friends
- Enhance self awareness

What would you like to learn?

____

____

Expectations:

- Relaxation/free time
- Fun
- Travel
- More time with family
- Some form of work
- Hobbies
- Financial security
- Socialize more
- Fitness
- Volunteering

What fits for you?

____

____

Concerns/Fears:

- Loneliness
- Boredom
- Illness
- Isolation
- Not enough money

Your concerns/fears?

____

____

____

Your fantasies?

____

____

____

THE POWER OF A POSITIVE ATTITUDE

Ken Dychtwald, in his book *Age Wave,* says:

> Invariably, they told me that in their view, the most essential determinant of successful aging is attitude. Each of us has the difficult task of steering our own ship through the challenging waters of life. Although it's good to have a sound boat, with a good motor and comfortable sleeping quarters, your attitude is in control of the wheel throughout the journey.

Dychtwald cites many people in their 60s, 70s, and 80s who are running marathons, playing tennis, swimming, and even cycling for up to eight hours a day on a regular basis, sometimes every day.

Unfortunately, these active individuals are still in the minority; most North Americans let themselves go with age. This is a conditioned response more than a necessary one. In

Satisfaction in retirement is driven much more by attitudes and behaviour than by the amount of money in the bank.

the final analysis it can be attributed to a sedentary lifestyle. The average U.S. senior walks about 25 miles a year. Even the average Canadian senior, who walks about 75 miles a year, is lazy compared with the average Danish senior, at 265 miles a year. The most popular activity for people over 55 is watching television.

This time of life can be an adult stage of generativity and self-actualization. The people most satisfied with retirement are those who guide the next generation and get involved in volunteer work, coaching, community building, and meaningful activities that give back in some way. You get to be who you always wanted to be or really were and do what suits you best.

Retirement is a process and can be a series of starts and stops rather than a race across a finish line.

You now have the opportunity to do what you've dreamed of and be the person you want to be. Idleness, loafing, and mental inertia may not be how you want to reinvent yourself – not for too long, anyway.

PASSIVE VS. ACTIVE LEISURE

Satisfying activities are often challenging and require physical and/or intellectual energy and engagement. The Academy of Leisure Sciences suggests an activity is satisfying if:

- You have a real interest in the activity
- You feel challenged in some way
- You feel a sense of accomplishment
- It is complex enough that you are not bored
- You develop or maintain skills
- You become immersed and lose track of time
- You experience a sense of self-development
- It is not too expensive

> **I have all the money I need if I die before four o'clock.**
>
> ~HENNY YOUNGMAN

Watching TV, gambling, or marathon napping rarely meet these criteria. Avoid activities that you experience as purposeless, monotonous, predictable, and passive. Loneliness, boredom, and a craving for excitement are cited by researchers as the main factors in the huge increase in senior gambling.

Aim for what makes you excited, engaged, proud of yourself, satisfied, and stretched a bit. You may even meet some like-minded people and become part of a new community that reflects your values and interests.

A Scotiabank poll found that 86 per cent of pre-retirees plan to travel. Good start, but you will need a few more activities in your lifestyle planning. Lifestyle plans depend on your financial reality, the quality of your health, and the range of your imagination and sense of adventure.

YOUR LEGACY

Think about a cause or mission that is bigger than you are.

What legacy or contribution do you want to make?

____

____

____

____

____

A staggering 80 per cent of luxury travel in North America is purchased by those over 55, with convenience, security, and comfort, not the price tag, the key considerations.

CREATIVE RETIREMENT IDEAS

1. Wine tasting in France or Italy or Scotch whiskey tours on Isla, Scotland.
2. Study Spanish in Cuba or French in Quebec City.
3. Take an art or art history class.
4. Hike in Spain, England, on the Bruce Trail, or in the canyons of the Southwestern U.S.
5. Revisit a place where you used to spend time.
6. Go dog sledding in the Yukon.
7. Take an Italian or East Indian or vegetarian cooking class.
8. Check out spafinder.com and fantasize.
9. Organize a stay at a French chateau for yourself and a group of your friends.
10. Join a drama club, go to a movie festival, make a scrapbook for a child, or Skype a friend.
11. Start a blues/folk/rock jam night at a local venue.
12. Drive a car to Florida and get paid for it.
13. Study the Canadian Arctic. Send harmonicas to a school there.
14. Tour Southern California, New Mexico, and Arizona in a rented RV.
15. Coach softball, soccer, tennis, or curling.
16. Visit Saturday markets. Can or freeze vegetables and fruit.
17. Take line dancing or ballroom dancing.
18. Go on a river cruise or see the Arctic.
19. Do a home exchange with someone from Europe.
20. Help build a school in Nicaragua or excavate a site with archeologists.
21. Help fundraise for an orphanage in Haiti or India.
22. Learn to play the ukulele or another instrument.
23. Follow your favourite baseball team through spring training in Florida.
24. Get creative your way.

DREAMS DO COME TRUE

List big dreams and small ones, practical and outrageous.

Get creative; be daring and expansive.

Dream big. What is on your bucket list?

1. ______________________________
2. ______________________________
3. ______________________________
4. ______________________________
5. ______________________________
6. ______________________________
7. ______________________________
8. ______________________________
9. ______________________________
10. ______________________________
11. ______________________________
12. ______________________________
13. ______________________________
14. ______________________________
15. ______________________________
16. ______________________________
17. ______________________________
18. ______________________________
19. ______________________________
20. ______________________________

~Inspired by the movie *The Bucket List,* with Morgan Freeman and Jack Nicholson, which made popular the idea of making a wish list of what you want to do or experience before you die.

MAKING DREAMS REAL

Prioritize your dream list from Most to Least important to you.

Pick the top ten and figure out how to make them real goals.

DREAM	ACTION (WHAT, HOW, WHO, RESOURCES, HELP NEEDED)	TIME NEEDED	MONEY NEEDED	OTHER FACTORS (HEALTH, FAMILY, LEARNING, TIMING)
1.			$	
2.			$	
3.			$	
4.			$	
5.			$	
6.			$	
7.			$	
8.			$	
9.			$	
10.			$	

Take as many steps as you need for each dream to become real. Set goals to make them happen in your life.

VOLUNTEERING

In Canada, volunteering adds value to society – estimated to be more than $14 billion annually. As of 2015, approximately 12.7 million Canadians volunteered 2.5 billion hours per year. This is the equivalent of one million full-time jobs. About 28 per cent of volunteers are 55 and over.

THE ART OF FINDING YOUR VOLUNTEER GROUP

Why do we call retirement an art? After all, as many believe, you simply stop working. The answer is that, for many of us, this period of life is the first time we actually have the opportunity to create the life we want. There is no model for this period, no Uncle George or Aunt Josie to tell you the best school to go to or the best place to work with the best benefits. It is only you and your imagination. *That's* why we call it an art form.

Earlier in life we learned to recount our skills. Now we develop the capacity to connect with others and to gain first-order information (information derived directly from people), information that will become the basis of our decisions. This can be a crucial time to explore and investigate various non-profits where you might be interested in volunteering your services. Questions you might ask include:

1. How clear is the organization's mission and is it something I deeply believe in?
2. How could my skills and experience contribute to this cause?
3. Is the organization open to integrating new people?
4. Is there an orientation program for new volunteers and/or board members?
5. How does the organization propose to utilize my talents? Do I run the risk of getting stuck licking stamps while others make decisions?
6. Am I feeling enthusiastic and committed?

Think of yourself as an interviewer using your emotional and intellectual skills to make sure that the personal qualities you possess are the ones you will actually get to use.

This may require new emotional strengths, such as clarifying how and where your experience connects with the organization's mission. The clearer you are in understanding your interests, your working style, and your needs, the more likely your audience is to value you.

The vast majority of volunteers want to contribute to their community or cause. Sports, recreation, and social services get the most support. Common activities include fund raising and organizing events. Over one-third of retirees do some form of volunteer service.

QUESTIONS ABOUT VOLUNTEERING

1. Have you volunteered before?
2. What skills and interests could you bring to an organization as a volunteer?
3. What organizations/groups would you like to research or approach?
4. How much time realistically will you have to volunteer?
5. Have you visited where you may be contributing?
6. Have you met the people you'll be working with?
7. Do you know the expectations or job description?
8. Is there prior training and supervision?
9. Is there flexibility or a replacement if you cannot be there?
10. Is it safe, well-run, and well-organized?

> Retirement – we have this myth that you have entered a nirvana and you are forever happy. The truth is, a lot of people struggle with this.
>
> ~DR. AMY D'APRIX, GERONTOLOGIST

A WORD TO MEN ON RETIREMENT

To avoid the potholes and pitfalls around retirement, read Lyndsay Green's book *Ready to Retire?* She opens with the D's that can create fear and dread about retirement: drink, depression, dementia, divorce, and death. Retirement may be perceived and experienced as a great source of loss by many: loss of identity, meaning, routine, colleagues, sense of purpose, status, respect, structure, the provider role, intellectual stimulation, and income. Replacing or adjusting to that loss can be daunting.

Green also interviews men who go looking for a new life of meaning and depth during retirement years. Those who do not reinvent themselves may need support and counselling to get unstuck and move forward with their lives. Many struggle with an existential crisis at some point.

Mitch Antony, author of *The New Retirementality*, suggests that men need a sense of purpose in retirement and non-stop leisure activities like golf do not do that.

Those who lose their positions, are downsized, or are pushed out have the hardest adjustment as they deal with so many emotions. Those who choose the timing of their retirements, leave on their own terms, and have written the final chapter of their career lives fare much better than those who do not.

The high suicide rate for aging men signals a real need for attention to the mental health and well-being of men in retirement.

Be mindful of spousal relationships so that you do not create the retired husband syndrome with your partner if you have one. The sandwich generation or club sandwich generation also adds stress with adult children, grandchildren, and aging parents needing help and support at the same time.

To improve the experience of retirement, start by seeding new activities, social connections, routines, and interests prior to retirement. Life enrichment while still working makes the adjustment smoother. Have something to retire to and look forward to. A list of to-dos can be over fairly quickly, so put in place what will sustain you over the hump of the transition period to the new life reality.

Continued personal growth, social engagement, good self-esteem, healthy relationships, a sense of humour, a fitness and health routine, and a proactive approach to retirement pay off in a better quality of life.

The model of the "men's sheds" from Australia and New Zealand is now in Canada. Check them out.

Men's book groups, walking groups, breakfast clubs, pub nights, and dining groups are springing up. Start a ROMEO group (Retired Old Men Eating Out). The local pub, BBQ, and party guys in my town are known as the Meat Eating Bastards.

The majority of men do only the financial planning for retirement. Lifestyle planning, psychological readiness, social networks, and a reinvention plan can make the world of difference. This is the most profound transition for most men and deserves time and attention.

Figure out how to have fun and make your time count.

Road Scholar Canada offers short-term academic courses at universities and colleges in 60 foreign countries.

LIFESTYLE ✓ CHECKLIST

- ☐ I have an idea how I want to celebrate my retirement
- ☐ I have a plan for my retirement honeymoon
- ☐ I have considered how I will structure my time
- ☐ I have hobbies and interests I intend to continue
- ☐ I have hobbies and interests I would like to try
- ☐ I have thought about starting a business or getting a part-time job
- ☐ I have made my bucket list
- ☐ I have considered options for volunteering
- ☐ I have looked at options for relocating
- ☐ I have some travel plans
- ☐ I am confident my financial resources match my lifestyle expectations
- ☐ I have a social network I can rely on
- ☐ I have discussed with my family how I want to live in retirement

I always seemed to have time or money – never both at the same time.
In retirement, I have a bit of both.
As long as I keep that balanced, I'll be fine.

~A RECENT RETIREE

Section Five

Relationships

RELATIONSHIP TIPS AND FACTS

YIKES, THERE'S A SPOUSE IN THE HOUSE!

Studies show that men and women fight more about money than any other topic. Are you ready for twice the spouse on half the money?

Communication is the key:

- Begin talking to each other about retirement as early as possible prior to retirement. This should begin no later than when the children are in university or out on their own. Even earlier would be better because it takes time to plan and build financial security and lots of time to allow for flexibility in your plans
- Be more open and frank with each other than you have ever been during your marriage. This may be very difficult at the beginning, especially if verbal communication has been a problem. Once you overcome this barrier, it will be much easier for you to work together to plan for the future
- All decision-making discussions should be carried on in private, away from the influence of others
- Many people say that a fun and perhaps best way to begin is for both the husband and wife to independently prepare a list of things they would like to do when retirement comes. Comparing the lists may show remarkable like-mindedness and some common ground or some eyebrow-lifting and perplexing surprises. For many couples this is where and how the whole openness process begins. Often, at this point, couples begin to realize that retirement planning is not just financial planning but a package with many dimensions
- Deal with the most pleasing and least controversial topics first. It will be easier to handle the sticky ones later
- Keep a watchful eye for something that may be troubling your spouse. Problems can impede free-flowing discussions. A husband may betray signs that he equates retirement to being old, or a wife that the effects of menopause have made her feel less attractive. Unless you subtly, sensitively, and diligently work at relieving your spouse's apprehension, this type of problem can destroy the positive attitude

so necessary to the development of your future plans. If you can't handle it, seek professional advice

- If you haven't yet learned to compromise, learn how now, because it's unlikely that what each of you wants out of retirement will coincide precisely. Don't ever try to intimidate or con your spouse where a major decision is concerned, unless you are willing to live with an unhappy mate whose vocabulary includes a constant, "I told you so, but you wanted to do it anyway"
- If you are a couple who wants to be in each other's company as much as possible, as you were before retiring, that's fine. However, don't be reluctant to give your spouse privacy to do things on his or her own, or to go somewhere without you tagging along. Of course, retirement means togetherness, but not necessarily being glued to your mate in all circumstances
- Encourage each other in all endeavours; be cooperative, and don't be hypercritical about how your spouse performs his or her allotted household tasks – mind your own business
- Retirement alters the ground rules of relationships; it's time to recalibrate
- Use this time to get to know your spouse/friends in a whole new way
- Roles may vary or at least be adjusted, especially if retirement happens at different times for each person
- Listening skills and respect continue to be important
- Compare values, plans, expectations, gripes
- Grandparenting or other connections with children may be very rewarding
- Beware of "turf" wars. In some cases the husband, having lost his turf at work, takes over his wife's
- Many men and women of 60, 70, and 80 years of age cohabit without the benefits of legal marriage
- Keep an eye on your marriage – both the romantic and the business sides. Spiralling legal fees and splitting assets can wreck retirement plans
- Flowers, bubble baths, good wine, candles, and Leonard Cohen's music can still work!
- A Cornell University study found that working women with retired or disabled husbands were the least happy while working men with retired wives were most happy

- A survey of Quebec retirees by TD Waterhouse found that scarcely half (52 per cent) of married retirees had the same vision of retirement as their spouse. Diverging dreams can lead to problems in retirement, when couples spend far more time together; 19 per cent said they experience conflict in their relationship
- "Retirement creates a whole new dynamic for couples who have spent years together in the same comfortable routine of going to work and raising kids," says relationship therapist Joe Rich, MSW, RSW. "There is an adjustment period that most couples experience when that routine changes. Getting ready emotionally to deal with that new reality can be tougher than people think, but talking to each other about your retirement expectations – and fears – can help to work through any issues, together"

A stable, harmonious marriage provides social, financial, and emotional resources and reduces stress. A bad relationship, however, can be worse than no relationship. People in conflict-ridden marriages have the highest levels of emotional loneliness and are particularly susceptible to physical health risks like heart disease, stroke, and diabetes.

Women in marriages strained with hostility are more likely to have elevated blood pressure and higher levels of stress hormones like cortisol; men suffer high blood pressure and angina. Immune and hormonal systems suffer, along with the ability to heal. We need validation from our loved ones for emotional security and a sense of well-being.

To add to the stresses, some parents well into their 70s are still giving some form of care to their children or step-children. In the 55 to 64 age group, 52 per cent of mothers and 42 per cent of fathers were providing some help to their adult children. StatsCan reports that 11 per cent of retired Canadians were still caregiving in some manner. In some cases adult children are still living in the family home having never left, or as boomerang children.

StatsCan further reports that about one in eight adult Canadians are providing some form of care to people with long-term health problems. This can be a sandwich generation squeeze that and puts pressure on families and increases stress.

I have spoken to many approaching retirement who are scared about what this means for their marriages. Some are apprehensive about the "Honey, I'm home every day now" announcement. About 62 per cent of partners disagree about timing of retirements, and only 32 per cent of couples communicate their visions of retirement beforehand.

Sharing, negotiating, compromising, and adjusting are not every couple's strong points. Integrating two lives in one space while dealing with identity shocks, loss of roles, and much more together time can be challenging. Therapists suggest advance planning, clear communication, compromise, patience, and clarification of expectations of each other and of retirement.

THE IMPORTANCE OF STAYING IN TOUCH

Researchers find a strong link between health and a strong sense of well-being and quality of life, on the one hand, and strong and high-quality social relationships and community engagement, on the other. In fact, isolation and loneliness can increase the risk of Alzheimer's and depression.

At age 75-plus, 64 per cent of women are widows. The overwhelming proportion of widows do not remarry or cohabit.

Keeping strong contacts with friends and family is especially important to the one-third or more of all seniors who live alone.

Don't count on your kids being fully independent despite RESPs, launched careers, or their marriages. Boomerang children, or crises experienced by your adult children, could be a drain on your personal and financial resources.

You may need to incorporate immediate and extended family and their needs and expectations into your retirement plans.

Your friends and community have an impact on plans, as well, especially if you intend to move closer to children or away from previous social networks.

- Strengthen bonds with your circle of friends, families, or partner
- Learn to ask for and accept help from family, friends, or professionals
- Remember the link between well-being and health and the quality of social relationships and community involvement
- Focus on new and old friendships; look up some of your previous contacts and see how they're doing now
- Remember, you will be dealing with grief and loss as Alzheimer's, illness, relocation, or terminal illness erodes your connections
- Cultivate family connections or friendships with younger people. Hanging out with little children can be fun, unless you are a W.C. Fields type: "Anyone who hates dogs and children can't be all bad"

- The happiest retirees are active and have many positive people in their lives – some older, some younger, and some the same age
- A key mistake for many is overestimating the impact of material possessions and underestimating the effect of social connections

GRAY DIVORCE

- More and more of the over-50 crowd are getting divorced, often after long-term marriages. Sometimes the split has been in the works for a long time or it may be a big surprise to one partner. Either way, the separation process is likely to be a wrenching and difficult one
- Both parties will need to work at maintaining family and friend connections
- Certified Divorce Financial Analysts can act as mediators and planners. They can refer to other professionals to keep the process as civil and simple as possible
- A volcano of emotions can cloud judgement. A divorce plan worked out with an objective and skilled advisor can keep everyone on track. Division of pensions and what happens to the house can be emotional triggers
- The transition to retirement requires a shared vision and lots of negotiations. At times, these negotiations fail. A majority of couples disagree on timing alone, and then it is twice the spouse on half the money! Do you stay and fight it out or give up and start over with what remains of your time on earth?
- The second, most popular reason for retirees going to a counsellor is relationship strain. It is not always with a spouse but too often is
- Be careful of splitting your assets with your legal team rather than your spouse. Figure out the best way to compose the last chapter of your marriage story. Getting divorced takes time to sort out assets, wants, needs, wishes, and effects on other family members. It requires careful management as it will echo through the rest of your lives
- Decisions need to be made about housing; distribution and possible sale of assets; pensions, benefits, debt, estate planning, and tax implications; and effects on retirement lifestyle for each party
- Bear in mind that a single person needs two-thirds of a couple's income to maintain the same lifestyle

- Choose experienced professionals who understand your values, instructions, and concerns
- The ability to communicate clearly, negotiate, and compromise can save time and effort as you work your way to a settlement that will preserve wealth
- Adult children and friends may react in ways you may not anticipate
- The common positives after a divorce are freedom, independence, and a separate identity with a new start while the negatives are loneliness and financial instability. Keep an eye on the bottom line if you want to go shopping to celebrate
- About 58 per cent of divorced women remarry, and 70 per cent of men do. Many couples choose common-law relationships or are LATs, "living apart together," as each has a separate home
- Read *When Harry Left Sally* by Marion Korn and Eva Sachs

HEADS UP

Replacing work colleagues with another network is just one of several pieces of advice from experts on how to transition well. Doing something meaningful is another.

Studies have found that if you have invested yourself in your career, you could feel depressed and empty in retirement. You need to rest and recover and then re-vision your future.

Negative effects of retirement can be a decline in physical activity, social interaction, and self-esteem. Factors that mitigate these effects include a strong marriage, social support, part-time work, and establishing a physical activity routine. Generally, however, retirees have lower stress and exercise more than their working counterparts.

> I do not claim to pass on any secret of life, for there is none, or any wisdom except the passionate plea of caring ... Try to feel, in your heart's core, the reality of others. This is the most painful thing in the world, probably, and the most necessary.
>
> ~MARGARET LAURENCE

Sharing decisions and information about health, finances, and legacy with adult children *may* be helpful. Powers of attorney for finances and personal care need to be in place and understood. A living will or enduring power of attorney needs to be available in case of an emergency, as well.

A WORD TO WIDOWS AND WIDOWERS

Just as chemo brain has patients struggling with memory and decision-making, widow or widower's brain can be problematic, too.

Trauma and grief can cause a kind of amnesia to protect the person from the pain of the loss. This causes forgetfulness, disorientation, confusion, poor decision-making, sleep problems, fatigue, outbursts of anger or crying, and even PTSD. It makes challenging, at best, all the decisions required about finances, housing, estate settlement, and more.

Other family members who are also dealing with their own grief may not react well, either. Family dynamics can become difficult. Decisions about home and estate can appear overwhelming to someone in the brain fog of grieving. Conflicts can arise when people are least able to cope.

Jennifer Black and Janet Baccarani, financial advisors as well as mother and daughter, have a short, readable book called *Managing Alone* that may be helpful. They also host a site, widowed.ca, where information is available. With 5 percent of Canadians losing partners to death each year, preparation and information can help.

God, grant me the senility
To forget the people I never liked anyway,
The good fortune to run into the ones I do,
And the eyesight to tell the difference.

ON YOUR OWN

More retirees than ever before are single. Most people can expect to be single for some part of their retirement, because of separation, divorce, or the death of a spouse.

Some prefer the independence of singlehood. Others join singles clubs, dating services, or dining clubs, place newspaper ads, and consult counsellors or an Internet site like seniorsmatch.com or so many similar sites. Some date as a hobby while others are seeking a long-term committed relationship.

We all need a balance of privacy and solitude as well as companionship and a sense of company. Relationships enrich and complicate our lives with intimacy, disappointment, love, support, and heartbreak. Relax and have fun whether you're single or not.

The 2011 Census tells us that about 43 per cent of seniors are single along with 31 per cent of the total population that is projected to get to 50 per cent by 2031. The seniors group includes the never married at 5 per cent, the separated or divorced at 8 per cent and rising, and the widows and widowers at 30 per cent. These are part of a growing trend to single living in Canada.

Taking a couple's income and dividing by two doesn't work for singles as they need two-thirds of a couple's income to keep the same lifestyle.

The number of singles shows up in travel, as well, with 35 per cent of Canadians travelling as singles, with more women than men going solo. Victoria, B.C., boasts a Women's Travel meetup group with over 500 members.

If planning retirement on your own, start earlier and review often. While still working make sure insurance is in place for a disability and also consider critical care insurance. Remember, RRSPs are taxed on withdrawal; save also with TFSAs and non-registered investments. No income splitting, no fall-back income earner, no sharing of expenses — any of these makes saving and tax planning even more important.

I think, therefore I'm single.

~Liz Winston

Beware those who woo for selfish purposes. The nurse or purse or sugar daddy scenario is very real as some take advantage of romantic relationships for monetary gain. Prenuptial agreements or cohabitation agreements can keep practical considerations clear as can direct communications about assets, attitudes to money, and spending patterns. Some are trying out the LAT (Living Apart Together) route where each maintains a separate household and bank accounts but are a couple otherwise.

The dating scene is booming for online over-50 sites. Sales of Viagra and Cialis are robust. Public health workers talk about the silent epidemic of sexually transmitted diseases among the older population. They are the pre-AIDS group who did not get the no-glove-no-love message regularly. They are also from the sex, drugs, and rock-and-roll generation and the beat goes on.

At retirement, singles need to stay socially active as common feelings of identity loss and loneliness can be difficult to overcome alone. Avoid a couch potato lifestyle by making efforts to be active and involved. Go find your people, hang out, do stuff, have fun, and carry on.

> Friendship with oneself is all important because without it one cannot be friends with anyone else.
>
> ~ELEANOR ROOSEVELT

RELATIONSHIP ✓ CHECKLIST

- ❑ I have strong social networks
- ❑ I have clear communications with my partner, children, and other family members
- ❑ I am a good listener
- ❑ I can listen with empathy
- ❑ I have friends from different age groups
- ❑ I understand my needs for intimacy and communicate them
- ❑ I have social supports that I can call on if I need to do so
- ❑ I understand my needs and those of my loved ones for independence, privacy, socializing, and support
- ❑ I feel connected to my community and neighbourhood
- ❑ I understand the importance of trust and mutual respect in a relationship
- ❑ I have a plan to stay in touch with those from work I want to keep in my life
- ❑ I know the importance of body language and non-verbal signals. I pay attention to these cues
- ❑ I am assertive and confident in my communications
- ❑ I manage my stress levels and emotions in order to improve my communications
- ❑ I communicate with trusted advisors for finances and health regularly and as needed
- ❑ I am available for friends and family but maintain my own boundaries
- ❑ I use a range of means of communication from social media, telephone, text, and snail mail to Skype or FaceTime

Section Six

Transitions

TRANSITIONABILITY TIPS AND FACTS

"Frankly, I don't know how I ever found the time to work." This is a common comment in retirement. However, some people are bored with the inactivity, devastated by their loss of identity, or actually fall into a state of depression.

Try to understand your inner feelings as you move from the known and comfortable – your work situation – to the unknown and often uncomfortable. Identity change can represent a serious loss.

Your private inner feelings will govern how successfully you cope with and adjust to the multitude of changes that retirement brings. A penthouse condominium on the ocean in Palm Beach, a packed schedule of leisure activities, and so on have very little meaning for people who are not pleased with themselves.

The real world of retirement consists of the same conflicting and perplexing emotional experiences you have always had: joy and sorrow, love and hate, hope and fear, contentment and stress, success and failure, satisfaction and dissatisfaction, togetherness and loneliness, and so on.

Retirement can be seen as a shift from a goal-oriented existence to a reflective one, a period when you can carefully consider the quality, meaning, and purpose of your life. It is not an escape or a long holiday. It is an opportunity to reinvent, reprioritize, and change life direction to match personal values.

When you retire, for the first time in your life you are largely free to follow the wishes and instincts of the natural rhythms of your mind and body. This is the time for the Maslow hierarchy's top level – self-actualization.

LOST IN TRANSITION

Retirement coaches and counsellors deal with many reactions to retirement and can help with preparation. Mariella Vigneux of Crabapple Consulting coaches, gives workshops, and does retirement-transition consulting. Here is her approach to retirement:

> Having worked as a professional coach since 2006, I've seen many reactions to retirement. I remember talking to a man who repeatedly refused to retire because he couldn't

imagine waking up each day with nothing to do. I met another person who had been retired for 40 years, yet was still talking about who he had been before retirement. One person told me she desperately wanted to retire – immediately – but strongly believed she'd be dead within a month if she did.

Retirement gets people asking themselves the big questions: Who will I become, apart from my professional identity? What will replace my daily routines when I no longer have work to dictate a clear direction? How do I ensure a happy, healthy and meaningful retirement, free from the resistance and anxiety that comes with radical change in lifestyle and diminished self-esteem?

Instead of retiring into a black hole or refusing to retire because you can't imagine a satisfying alternative, consider preparing ahead of time. Begin dreaming. Begin thinking about your new identity, as well as the exceptional opportunities possible in your retirement. Practise retiring. Build an implementation plan – from career resignation, through transition, and into your early retirement days. Then sit back and watch the fun unfold.

Through professional coaching, retirement workshops, and retirement transition consulting, Mariella focuses on emotional and social well-being in retirement. She offers a monthly newsletter, filled with personal retirement stories, thoughts about living and aging well, and retirement stats and studies. She says her job delights her constantly.

IDENTITY CRISIS

- People relate to you differently than at the workplace. Self-esteem may suffer, and the change can cause adjustment difficulties. This can happen very soon after retirement or after the honeymoon period is over – usually six months to two years after retirement
- A counsellor can help negotiate this potential psychological minefield. A mentor is invaluable as a sounding board and source of reassurance through this challenging transition
- This issue of identity takes the most people to a counsellor after retirement. The second one, by the way, is relationships. It's estimated that about 40 per cent of the workforce is afraid to retire. What are they afraid of?
- Retirement can bring on an existential crisis as questions about purpose and meaning come to the fore

- Loss of a sense of self is associated with retirement. Many identify with their jobs as who they are and the void of retirement looms for them
- The higher the level of responsibility, the more difficult the transition. Those achievers feel the loss of status, social connections, routine, and responsibility. "People needed me and what I did was important, but now what?"
- The Japanese term for death by overwork is *karoshi* and demanding corporate culture can result in death from overwork, poor lifestyle, and continuous high stress levels. The other risk is suicide as many early retirees, executives in particular, feel junked or rejected by their employers or do not move on to reinvent themselves in retirement
- Many associate retirement with mortality and the last stage of their lives. This is part of the "put out to pasture" belief that does not bode well for a positive, active retirement
- Others experience a grief period for the loss of their former selves and the positive feedback and sense of accomplishment that came with working
- Watch out for sleep problems, weight gain or loss, moodiness and anger, depression, social isolation, high-risk behaviours like gambling, drinking to excess, drug abuse, or sexual acting out. These are not good coping methods for filling a void or establishing a new sense of identity
- Recreating a new routine and schedule, a new sense of purpose and community can be a huge challenge. That is why planning ahead can reduce or avoid the effects altogether. Put some alternative activities and goals in place for the first two years of retirement at least
- Ask for help before it is a full-blown personal crisis. Dealing with transitions as profound as this one often requires a mentor, coach, or counsellor
- Read *Ready to Retire?* by Lyndsay Green, who interviewed a number of men and some of their spouses who share their experiences candidly. It is a comprehensive, honest, and enlightening look at the experience of retirement
- Switching from being fully engaged with your career to a nearly idle retiree is a recipe for personal disaster

SECRETS OF THE SUCCESSFULLY RETIRED

How do successfully retired people maintain their well-being and continue to make contributions to all facets of life?

1. *They face reality.*
   In other words, they have learned to accept life as it is and to make the best of it. They are not afraid to compromise when necessary.
2. *They take responsibility.*
   They do not blame others for their problems. They can accept help when it is needed, but they also make a major effort to solve their own problems.
3. *They are interested in other people.*
   They do not withdraw from life. They like doing things with and for other people. They make the effort to make new friends. They like their old friends, but they also like to keep in touch with younger people.
4. *They have strong and varied interests.*
   Well-adjusted persons usually like to engage in many kinds of activities, and they enjoy sharing activities with other people.
5. *They are interested in new things.*
   Most of them agree that the world is changing faster than they can comprehend, but they still try to keep up with things. They are not afraid of the future, and they accept changing times.
6. *They look forward to the future.*
   They live in the present and the future instead of in the past. At least some of the things they can reasonably expect to accomplish are projected into the future.
7. *They monitor their health.*
   Well-adjusted people take the initiative to achieve good health. They do not dwell on their aches and pains.

I am an old man and have known a great many troubles,
but most of them never happened.

~MARK TWAIN

8. *They pay attention to their appearance.*
   They take pride in their appearance, and they usually have a strong interest in keeping the place in which they live in good order.

9. *They know how to relax and enjoy.*
   Happily retired people know how to relax and do not take life too seriously. Pleasure is the key to health and the essence of living fully. People who have not developed resources for enjoyment tend to experience life – and especially aging – as a burden.

10. *They roll with the punches.*
    One of the strongest assets possessed by successful retirees is an ability to change and adapt their ideas, habits, and attitudes as the situation requires it. Flexibility is the key.

WALKING THE TALK

- How's your attitude today?
- Don't walk away from negative people – *run*!
- Keep focused on your needs and your goals
- Maintain a balance between active and passive activities
- Generate many ideas for living, keep reimagining
- If you're bored, remember who is causing it
- Don't miss the moment; master it
- The ultimate goal is enjoying the process and savouring the journey
- Be spontaneous
- Dare to be different
- Take a risk
- Solitude is for secure people
- Laugh and be silly
- The best things in life are free

- Keep physically fit
- Avoid excessive TV watching and other screens
- Keep mentally fit
- Goof off at times
- Develop your spiritual side
- Beware of addictions, depression, and envy, and work on becoming the best you can be
- Make a positive difference

HOW TO MANAGE THE FIRST YEAR

1. Beware of time poachers who volunteer you because they assume you have nothing to do. Learn to say no; stay flexible as you choose how you want to spend your time. Activity addiction is going around and around in smaller and smaller circles just for the sake of being busy. The first is voluntoldism, the second, busyholism.
2. "Drift time" allows serendipity, curiosity, mind clearing, new experiences, and time to exhale. Allow some time to yourself, keep things simple, and sort out what's next while you shift gears.
3. Negotiate personal time and personal space with your housemates.
4. Connect with other retirees and find a mentor or two or a few friends who can guide you through the transition period.
5. Maintain your sense of humour and perspective.

> One reason the transition can be difficult for some people is that retirement really is not one, but many, transitions. Our work, after all, gives us an identity. It maps out routines, our relationships. Work very often is, in effect, our community.
>
> ~NANCY SCHLOSSBERG, *RETIRE SMART, RETIRE HAPPY*

6. Beware of the impulse itch. For example: Now that I'm not working, I can renovate the house, redo the gardens, take courses, go out to dinner and theatre, build a shed, take a couple of trips ... You're likely to find yourself broke and exhausted. Take your time. You don't have to do it all in the first year.
7. Keep a diary or journal so you can sort through your days in a mindful way. Then review that first year at the first anniversary of your retirement. Figure out what went well and what can be left behind, what the dead ends were and the opportunities to build again.
8. The transitions continue as circumstances, relationships, health, energy levels, and attitudes change.
9. Figure out your new routine, the new structure to your day, week, and year.
10. Find new purpose for your life.
11. Establish new communities, groups, and individuals to interact with and fit them into new routines.

ATTITUDE IS EVERYTHING

NEGATIVITY THRIVES ON:

Rumour
Gossip
Lack of information
Anger, resentment
Lack of trust
Personal issues
Low morale
Blaming

> Life isn't fair, but it's still good.
>
> ~REGINA BRETT, 90 YEARS OF AGE

Scapegoating
Lack of control
Frustration
Lack of energy

NEGATIVITY IS TAMED BY:

Trust
Openness, honesty
Communication
Accurate information
Increased empowerment
Celebration
Positive solutions
Positive attitude
Facing/confronting fears
Outlet for fear
Honour and respect
Confidentiality

> Being "over the hill" is much better than being under it.
> ~BARRY HOPKINS, AUTHOR OF
> THE NEWSPAPER COLUMN "SMILE PILE"

IT'S NOT JUST BETTY WHITE

1. A 95-year-old former newspaper columnist in Worcester, Massachusetts, Jane Goyer, sold her first book for publication to Harper & Row Publishers.
2. At 95, Bertrand Russell was actively promoting international world peace.
3. Mother Teresa was active helping the poor through her Missionaries of Charity until her death.
4. At 90, Picasso was still creating drawings and engravings.
5. Linus Pauling, a two-time Nobel laureate, was active at 90 looking for new benefits of taking mega doses of vitamins.
6. Luella Tyra was 92 in 1984 when she competed in five categories at the United States Swimming Nationals in Mission Viejo, California.
7. Lloyd Lambert at 87 was an active skier and running a 70-plus ski club with 3,286 members, including a 97 year old.
8. Maggie Kuhn, at 83, was still active in promoting the goals of the Gray Panthers, a seniors group that she helped found when she was 65.
9. Buckminster Fuller in his 80s was actively promoting his vision for a new world.
10. Harvey Hunter of Edmonton, while celebrating his 104th birthday, was asked about the secret of a long life. He replied,"Keep breathing!" Harvey became a volunteer when he was 90 and started university at 91.
11. Vera Mackenzie of Penticton, B.C., volunteered at Parkway Elementary School on Fridays at 100 years old.
12. John Tomczak of Victoria, B.C., volunteered at Victoria Hospice at 92.
13. Mickey Rooney at 90 was still performing his songs and stories.
14. Alice Munro won the Nobel Prize for Literature August 2016 at age 82.
15. Frank Lloyd Wright designed the Guggenheim Museum at age 90.
16. Leonard Cohen released a new album in August 2016 at age 82. He had performed 470 shows over five years between ages 76 and 81.

ADVICE FROM THOSE WHO'VE GONE BEFORE

1. Create new social networks.
2. Allow yourself to play often.
3. Follow your creative instincts.
4. Continue to learn.
5. Don't take yourself too seriously.
6. Listen to others. It's the best gift you can give.
7. Find folks to do nothing with and hang out with them.
8. Be careful of parking yourself in front of a TV, computer, or slot machine.
9. Figure out what you want to leave behind – your legacy, your gift(s) to your family, community, country, and planet.

REGRETS – I'VE HAD A FEW

Common themes at the end of life include:

1. Many people say they wish they'd lived their lives true to themselves rather than reacting to the expectations of others. Too many dreams go unpursued and unfulfilled for too long.
2. Men in particular often regret spending so much time at work that they missed their children's successes and experiences, their own friendships, and opportunities to connect with others. They stayed on the treadmill of work and missed out on much.
3. Some people regret that they squelched their true feelings in order to keep peace. They harboured bitterness, anger, or resentment that poisoned their peace of mind.

> **Being retired is sort of like Grade Four – cooperative play, helping others, having and making friends, and learning lots.**
>
> ~ANONYMOUS

4. Many regret that they gave up friendships and connections. In the final analysis, love and relationships hold the greatest importance.
5. Some wish they had let themselves be happier, recognizing that happiness is a choice.

YOUR "I'M RETIRED NOW" INTRODUCTION

How to answer the inevitable question when you meet a new person.

I'm retired now but I used to ____________________

I left that behind because ____________________

Now I can ____________________

Optional additions (add two or three as conversation starters)

I really enjoy ____________________

I feel ____________________

I can't believe ____________________

I'm looking forward to ____________________

I'm interested in ____________________

I spend my time ____________________

I have discovered ____________________

> Life is a banquet and most fools are starving to death.
>
> ~ANONYMOUS

RETIREMENT – PUTTING IT ALL TOGETHER

1. Why are you planning retirement now? Consider your motivation.
2. Do you really want to retire? Why or why not?
3. Have you consulted retirement planning and financial planning experts or attended seminars?
4. Do you know your present financial picture and how it would change in retirement?
5. Have you considered or started community activities or interpersonal or personal endeavours you will pursue in retirement?
6. Have you researched or started new learning opportunities?
7. What are the reactions and expectations of your family and friends to your retirement and your plans?
8. Have you considered volunteer, part-time or temporary positions, or a small business venture?
9. What is important, what are you passionate about, and what do you value? How are these incorporated into your retirement plans?
10. Are you comfortable with your own identity, with uncertainty, and with exploring possibilities when it concerns your retirement?
11. Do you have a clear financial picture and plan?
12. Do you have a health, wellness, fitness plan?
13. Do you have a leisure-time plan?
14. Do you have social networks?
15. Do you have relationship renewal and/or renegotiation plan?
16. Have you set your priorities for:
    - Pre-retirement
    - Your retirement celebration
    - Your honeymoon period?
17. Do you have a sense of what the best timing would be for you?
18. Do you know your transition style?
19. Are you confident in your progress and your choices?

20. Are you supported in your choices?

21. Do you have a team of advisors who will work together for your benefit?

HAVE A DREAM

1. **HAVE A DREAM**
   - Create a vision for the future
2. **DEVELOP A PLAN**
   - Organize your thinking
3. **CONTROL YOUR FOCUS**
   - Don't do too many things at once
4. **TAKE PERSONAL INITIATIVE**
   - Act as if it all depends on you
5. **PRACTISE SELF-DISCIPLINE**
   - Don't be distracted, stay on target
6. **LEARN TO BUDGET**
   - Put your time, energy, and money behind your plan
7. **EVIDENCE ENTHUSIASM**
   - It's contagious
8. **ENJOY YOURSELF**
   - Laughter is healing
9. **GO FOR IT!**
   - Keep the faith no matter what

   (Adapted from Ian Percy's *The 11 Commandments for an Enthusiastic Team*)

Age is mind over matter. If you don't mind, it doesn't matter.

TRANSITIONS ✓ CHECKLIST

- ❑ I know the signs of low self-esteem, depression, and anxiety and will seek help if I need it
- ❑ I know transitions can be challenging to my identity, relationships, and routine
- ❑ I am looking forward to being retired
- ❑ I am confident in my coping skills to deal with this transition
- ❑ I have a positive attitude toward my future
- ❑ I have prepared myself to the best of my ability
- ❑ I have a sense of identity outside my work role
- ❑ I realize my sense of identity may be changing
- ❑ I have the resources and support I need to retire happily
- ❑ I have people to confide in when I need to talk
- ❑ I have plans I am looking forward to carrying out
- ❑ I have confidence in my ability to deal with whatever my future holds

Section Seven

Resources

ONLINE RESOURCES

ageonomics.ca

Lee Anne Davies shares insights on aging.

buildingwealth.ca

Resources on finances with Gordon Pape.

carp.ca

Canadian Association of Retired Persons, advocacy, Zoomer media, membership.

carpevitam.ca

Dr. Suzanne Cook site for educational purposes.

challengefactory.ca

Challenges outdated career thinking, end-to-end legacy career transition services.

cra-arc.gc.ca

Information, services, and forms for tax purposes.

crabapple.ca

Resources, workshops, retirement coaching.

donnamccaw.ca

Author's website.

eldertreks.com

Small group travel for 50-plus.

equifax.com

Check your credit rating.

findependencehub.com

Financial independence pointers.

getsmarteraboutmoney.ca

From the Ontario Securities Commission, calculators, tools, retirement planning.

imaginecanada.ca
Charitable organization, philanthropy.

journeywoman.com
Women's travel news.

meetup.com
Find interest groups in your area.

moneysense.ca
Many useful resources about finances.

myredirection.com
Dr. Suzanne Cook does research and advocacy for later life work and workers.

nutritionfacts.org
Food as preventive medicine by Dr. Michael Greger.

retirehappy.ca
Excellent resources on finances and lifestyle.

retirementadvisor.ca
Excellent tools, calculators, and insights.

roadscholar.org
Travel the world and learn with peers.

seniorshelpingseniors.com
Ask for help or offer help.

seniorsinfo.ca
Ontario Seniors' Secretariat.

senioryears.com
Resources and links for 50-plus.

servicecanada.gc.ca
Register and get your information on CPP.

solotravelerblog.com
Trips and tips for singles.

thirdquarter.ca or hire-experience.ca
Recruiter of those over 45, free of charge.

travel.gc.ca
Resources, warnings from Canadian government.

trustedhousesitters.com
An option for house and pet sitting while travelling.

victorylapretirement.com
Advantages of some employment income and engagement in retirement.

widowed.ca
Resources for the suddenly single.

BOOKS FOR FURTHER RESEARCH

Beyond Age Rage by David Cravit

Debt-Free Forever: Becoming a Woman of Independent Means by Gail Vaz-Oxlade

During Your Time of Loss: Information for Survivors by Service Canada

The Essential Retirement Guide by Fred Vettese

The Family Guide to Disability and Personal Finances by Ed Arbuckle; forthcoming, 2017

It's Your Money by Gail Vaz-Oxlade

The Laughing Boomer: Retire from Work — Gear up for Living! by Mahara Sinclaire

Living Apart Together: A New Possibility for Loving Couples edited by Linda Breault and Dianne Gillespie

Never Too Late by Gail Vaz-Oxlade

Pensionize Your Nest Egg by Moshe A. Milevsky and Alexandra C. Macqueen

The Perfect Home for a Long Life by Lyndsay Green

The Real Retirement: Why You Could Be Better Off Than You Think, and How to Make That Happen by Fred Vettese and Bill Morneau

Ready to Retire? What You and Your Spouse Need to Know About the Reality of Retirement by Lyndsay Green

Redefining Retirement: New Realities for Boomer Women by Dr. Margret Hovanec and Elizabeth Shilton

Retirement in Canada by Thomas R. Klassen

Retirement's Harsh New Realities: Protecting Your Money in a Changing World by Gordon Pape

Stayin' Alive: How Canadian Boomers Will Work and Play and Find Meaning by Michael Adams

The Third Rail by Jim Leech and Jacquie McNish

Victory Lap Retirement by Mike Drak and Jonathan Chevreau

The Wealthy Barber Returns by David Chilton

When Harry Left Sally: Finding Your Way Through Grey Divorce by Marion Korn and Eva Sachs

You Could Live a Long Time: Are You Ready? by Lyndsay Green

FILMS TO INSPIRE THINKING ABOUT AGING AND RETIREMENT

About Schmidt (2002)
Jack Nicholson is Warren Schmidt, a doleful 65-year-old retired insurance executive from Omaha who sets out on a desperate quest for meaning in an RV that his recently deceased wife had bought for travel in their golden years. Schmidt's encounters – with his daughter, his son-in-law, and his mother (Kathy Bates) – require the tolerance and mental flexibility he's previously not possessed. This is the all-time how-not-to-retire movie.

Amour (2012)
Unflinching and challenging look at love and aging.

Away from Her (2006)
Gordon Pinsent and Julie Christie in a touching Alzheimer's story.

The Best Exotic Marigold Hotel 1 (2011) and 2 (2015)
British retirees outsource their retirements to less expensive India and find adventures.

The Bucket List (2007)
Jack Nicholson and Morgan Freeman face their mortality with imagination and verve.

Danny Collins (2015)
Old rocker gets a long-lost letter and changes his ways.

Elsa and Fred (2014)
Never too late for romance, friendship, and adventure.

Grace and Frankie (2015-2016)
Jane Fonda, Lily Tomlin, Martin Sheen, Sam Waterston create a funny, human story. (Netflix TV series)

Gran Torino (2008)
Clint Eastwood's grumpy old man is not one to mess with.

Iris
Iris Murdoch, the unconventional British author of numerous popular novels and several works of philosophy, descends into Alzheimer's disease while her devoted husband, literary critic John Bayley, strives to sustain her. Their complex romance, told in flashbacks, is both poignant and provocative. Stars Judy Dench as the elderly Iris and Kate Winslet as the youthful Murdoch.

It's Complicated (2009)
Ex spouse becomes lover while being wooed by ... yes, it is complicated.

The Lady in the Van (2015)
A playwright befriends a homeless woman who parks a van in his driveway for 15 years.

Mr. Holmes (2015)
Near the end of his life, Sherlock tries to solve one more case despite his scrambled memory and fading skills.

Nebraska (2013)
Family thrown into crisis when dad decides to go on a crazy quest.

Quartet (2012)
A home for retired artists gets a new diva.

RED (Retired Extremely Dangerous) (2010), *RED 2* (2013)
Helen Mirren arranging flowers, Bruce Willis leading a quiet life in suburbia, John Malkovich in a bunker, Morgan Freeman in a seniors home all sounds so quiet. It's anything but ...

Remember (2015)
Holocaust revenge and revelation with a memory-loss twist.

Trouble with the Curve (2012)
Baseball scout has to ask for help from family to keep working.

The Visitor (2007)
Unexpected guests rekindle a joy for living.

The World's Fastest Indian (2005)
The life story of New Zealander Burt Munro (played by Anthony Hopkins), who in 1965, at age 68, risks everything, including his own life, by taking his vintage motorcycle to the Bonneville Salt Flats in Utah to break the world speed record.

Young @ Heart (2007)
Documentary about a choir of seniors that performs songs from Cold Play to Hendrix.

Youth (2015)
Two old friends holiday and reflect on their lives and work, whereupon surprises and opportunities pop up.

Best tip ever: get a library card – music, movies, computer use, printing, books, magazines, research resources – all free!

~RECENT RETIREE

Acknowledgements

Thank you to Don Bastian at BPS Books for his guidance and expertise. All the best with that semi-retirement!

To all the people I have learned from, worked with, and been inspired by in the work we do. These include Eleanor Ross, Robin Lee Norris, Jim Yih, Pam Katunar, Lyndsay Green, Mariella Vigneax, Pam McDonald, Bev Carter, Lisa Taylor, Dr. Sue Ferreira, Anne Day, and Mathieu Powell.

And to friends and family, who mean so much.

About the Author

Donna McCaw (B.A., M.Ed.) retired at age 54 after a career in education and counselling at high schools and colleges, including Adult Education programs. A master's degree in Applied Psychology, a joy for storytelling, and a wry sense of humour combine to make her an effective educator and entertainer. Her writing and presentations are straightforward, down to earth, and accessible as well as spirited and fun.

Donna has worked in arts and volunteer organizations, the business community, advocacy groups, and women's groups. As well, she has given presentations from keynotes to trainings to performances. She has written books and given readings, done storytelling, produced shows, and volunteered for many organizations, most recently with Save Our Water, working to protect local water from commercial water bottling.

Her mission is to inspire people to have the retirement they are passionate about with confidence in their decisions and choices. Since retiring, she has travelled from India to Italy, from Bali to the southern tip of Argentina, and from New Zealand to New Mexico. She has also helped to renovate a house on Vancouver Island, led Retirement Readiness and Women in Retirement courses, and generally learned to say yes to most opportunities.

Donna lives in Elora, Ontario.

TO ORDER THIS BOOK

Please go to one of the following:
bpsbooks.com
amazon.ca (Canada)
amazon.com (United States)
amazon.co.uk (United Kingdom)
Your local bookstore

TO ARRANGE

Speaking Engagements
Workshops
Courses
Retirement Lifestyle presentations
Women Around the Kitchen Table sessions
please go to the author's website, donnamccaw.ca

CPSIA information can be obtained
at www.ICGtesting.com
Printed in the USA
LVOW09s0740290317
528872LV00001B/1/P